The Complete Idiot's Reference Card

Top Ten Checklist for Writing the Perfect Cover Letter

Take a hard look at your letter to make sure you haven't forgotten anything. Get out your pencil and check off each of the following items.

❏ **1.** Your name appears in the letterhead in the top center or on the upper right-hand side (not in the upper left-hand corner) of the page.

❏ **2.** Your letter is addressed to the hiring manager, the Director of Human Resources, or to someone in the company who you personally know.

❏ **3.** Your letter starts with a strong lead sentence that engages the reader immediately.

❏ **4.** You quickly establish a personal connection with the reader by referencing a friend, associate, or area of interest common to you both.

❏ **5.** The text of your letter gives the reader a sense of your personality.

❏ **6.** Your letter sells the reader on the prospect of you working for him or her.

❏ **7.** The closing paragraph initiates a next step, such as an interview.

❏ **8.** Your cover letter refers to an enclosed resume.

❏ **9.** Your letter fits on one page and looks quick and easy to read.

❏ **10.** You have used good grammar and writing style throughout your letter.

alpha
books

The Four Rules of the Road for Writing the Perfect Cover Letter

1. **Establish a Personal Connection**

   Immediately make a connection with your reader with an attention-grabbing first line. Drop a familiar name, make a bold claim, ask a probing question, or incorporate a quotable quote.

2. **Show Personality**

   Give the employer a sense of your personality through your writing style, direct statements about your character, or testimonial references.

3. **Initiate Action**

   Tell the employer that you will contact him to take the next step (probably an interview) or, if you can't contact him, motivate him to contact you.

4. **Make It Quick and Easy to Read**

   Format your one-page letter using short paragraphs, bullet points, or columns to make your communication look quick and easy to read.

Cover Letter Dos and Don'ts

1. **Don't summarize your resume**

   Your letter should introduce and complement your resume, not repeat it!

2. **Don't write a form letter**

   Your letter should not sound like a form letter. Use a friendly, professional style of writing.

3. **Do avoid salary disclosure**

   Salary negotiations belong in the interview, not in your cover letter.

4. **Do proofread**

   Make sure there are no typos in your composition.

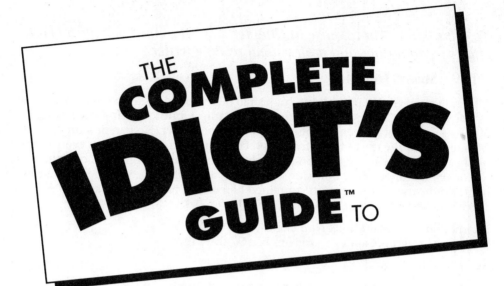

THE COMPLETE IDIOT'S GUIDE™ TO

the Perfect Cover Letter

by Susan Ireland

alpha books

A Division of Macmillan Reference USA
A Simon & Schuster Macmillan Company
1633 Broadway, New York, NY 10019

To Mom (alias Aunt Louise in Chapter 17), who has lovingly supported my efforts as an author and professional resume writer.

©1997 Susan Ireland

International Standard Book Number: 0-02-861960-9
Library of Congress Catalog Card Number: 97-073149

98 97   8 7 6 5 4 3 2 1

Interpretation of the printing code: the rightmost number of the first series of numbers is the year of the book's printing; the rightmost number of the second series of numbers is the number of the book's printing. For example, a printing code of 97-1 shows that the first printing occurred in 1997.

Printed in the United States of America

Senior Editor
Nancy Mikhail

Production Editor
Chris Van Camp

Copy Editor
Michael E. Cunningham

Cover Designer
Mike Freeland

Illustrator
Judd Winick

Designer
Glenn Larsen

Indexer
Greg Pearson

Production Team
Angela Calvert
Kim Cofer
Linda Knose
Maureen West

Contents at a Glance

Contents

Part 2: Your Resume Booster

Foreword

Psychologists and employers tell us that first impressions make all the difference in every aspect of life. And the first impression anybody is going to get of you in most job searches is your COVER LETTER!

That's why it has to be perfect. And now, with the help of Susan Ireland's practical suggestions and excellent samples, you can devise a strategy that makes employers want you! A good resume not "covered" by a catchy, customized, compelling letter will not get noticed the way you want it to—and will often not get read at all. Most employers spend less than ten seconds on their first perusal of a cover letter and resume, and it's a one-shot deal. So if you get into the "no thanks" file because your cover letter didn't catch the reader's interest in that first quick read-through, there's no way back from there.

But don't panic. *The Complete Idiot's Guide to the Perfect Cover Letter* takes you from your first attack of writer's block through the research and strategy stages right up to polishing the finished product. Susan Ireland will be with you all the way, anticipating sticky wickets like age, shifting fields, returning to the workforce, time out and the like, and showing you how to make that cover letter shine with the best of who you are!

So even if you resist "marketing yourself" (most people do—for some reason, they just expect to be "discovered" by employers), bite the bullet and let Susan Ireland be your coach. Look at it this way: The better your cover letter, the better the likelihood of an interview, the shorter the job search. Wouldn't you love to have this over with?

It's easy to see why you'd have to be a complete idiot not to do what this wise and witty book tells you to do!

Barbara B. Reinhold, Ed.D

Barbara B. Reinhold, Ed.D., Director, Career Development Office, Smith College. Also author of TOXIC WORK: How to Overcome Stress, Overload and Burnout, and Revitalize Your Career *(Dutton 1996/Plume 1997) and AW Career Coach on "About Work" on AOL and the Web.*

Introduction

You're stuck!

You've got a hot lead on a job opening; and you're all set to send your resume except for one thing—you need a cover letter. And you know it's got to be a winner (one that doesn't sound like a form letter) if you're going to convince the employer to call you for an interview.

And that's where you're stuck—coming up with a dynamite cover letter. You may assume cover letters are *supposed* to be dry and boring. Well, throw that theory out the window and follow the guidelines in this book. You'll be surprised how much license you have to express yourself in a letter, and what results that expression brings.

The Complete Idiot's Guide to the Perfect Cover Letter is going to lead you by the hand through the letter-writing process as you:

➤ Create a winning cover letter strategy

➤ Write each line to get the most out of your qualifications

➤ Look spiffy with a great format

➤ Distribute your new letter (and resume) to employers

Whether you're having trouble making the first mark on your page or you're stuck in the middle of composing your masterpiece, this book will help you come up with a terrific letter. To understand how, let's look at what's inside.

Part 1, "Before You Start," explains the two types of job search letters and how to decide which letter strategy is best for you. You'll also find in this section the "Four Rules of the Road"—my secrets for the perfect letter.

Part 2, "Your Resume Booster," is where you'll read about my straightforward, four-step cover letter-writing process. Before you know it, you'll have an outstanding cover letter ready to send out.

Part 3, "Getting the Right Message Into the Right Hands," tells you how to deal with tough cover letter issues (like responding to requests for your salary history) and what *not* to say in your letter. This part also gives practical advice on how to make your letter look handsome and where to send your resume/cover letter packet.

Part 4, "Other Hardworking Letters," shows you a creative way of combining the typical resume and cover letter to produce a powerful, one-page hybrid called a broadcast letter. You'll also find tips on how to write a request for an *informational interview* (a meeting with a professional to get career advice) and thank-you letters.

Part 5, "The ABCs of Good Writing Technique," covers the basics of style and grammar that will contribute to the professional impression of your letter. In case you're the type to get all tangled up in past participles, dangling modifiers, and all that technical stuff, turn to this section for quick relief. You'll also learn how to break through writer's block by using techniques that will help you let go of your inhibitions so you can deliver an effective message. And if your brain freezes over at the mention of "letter writing," this section will thaw it out.

The Appendix contains a portfolio of dynamite cover letters. What better way to grasp the concepts of powerful letter writing than to see effective samples!

If you're like most job hunters, you've put off writing your letter until the last minute; or maybe you just learned about a job opportunity and want to jump on it right away. In either case, don't worry! You'll meet your deadline if you just relax and follow my letter-writing steps one at a time.

And even though you know you'll *never* procrastinate again (ahem!), think of how much *less* time it will take the next time you have to write a letter the night before.

Signposts Along the Way

You'll notice the following sidebars throughout the book. They mark some special points I want you to be sure to catch.

Q & A

These sidebars contain typical questions asked by job seekers and answers from an experienced job counselor—me!

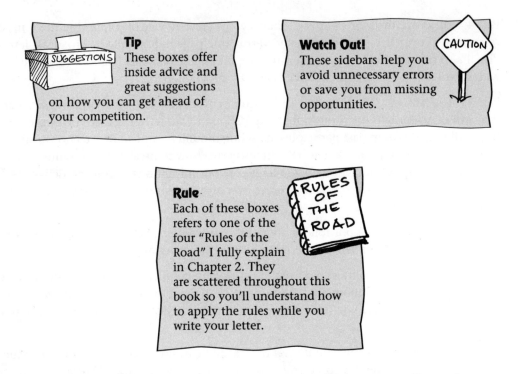

Tip
These boxes offer inside advice and great suggestions on how you can get ahead of your competition.

Watch Out!
These sidebars help you avoid unnecessary errors or save you from missing opportunities.

Rule
Each of these boxes refers to one of the four "Rules of the Road" I fully explain in Chapter 2. They are scattered throughout this book so you'll understand how to apply the rules while you write your letter.

Susan Ireland's Cover Letter and Resume Service

Writing Service: From anywhere in the United States, you can get your cover letter and resume written professionally through Susan Ireland's Resume Writing Service. One of my associates will compose and produce your resume and cover letter, working with you by phone, fax, e-mail, and mail. For those of you who live in the San Francisco area, you can get your resume and letter written during a one-on-one session.

Critique Service: If you've already written your cover letter and resume, use Susan Ireland's Resume Critique Service to be sure you have the most effective job search tools possible. A professional resume writer will examine your letter and resume, and give you a critique by phone. (Believe me, we pack a lot of information into our critique sessions.)

For information about Susan Ireland's Cover Letter and Resume Service, call (510) 558-0632.

Acknowledgments

My gratitude to the following people who helped me write this book. Ruth Schwartz (who contributed cover letters she had written and lent her editorial support), Beth Brown (who contributed cover letters she had composed), Yana Parker (for mentoring me in resume writing), Tad Gage (for his brainstorming and editorial support), Bob Moon (for his advice and support), André Abecassis (my literary agent from Anne Elmo Agency), my editorial/production team at Macmillan Reference: Nancy Mikhail (Senior Editor), Chris Van Camp, (Production Editor), Michael Cunningham (Copy Editor), and Greg Pearson (Indexer), and others who offered me their support: Jane Conger, Pauline Iliff, and my colleagues at Alumnae Resources career center in San Francisco. Thank you all!

Part 1
Before You Start

The hiring manager leans intently over the paperwork on his desk to examine job candidate qualifications for the "millionth" time. The competition for a particular job has come down to two candidates—you and a fellow with just about equal experience. Suddenly the manager sits up straight and smiles. There's no question which person he wants to hire—you! He has favored you right from the start when you sent that personable letter; and you ensured that the rapport grew with each proceeding step in the application process. You're the one he wants on his team because he likes you!

The above scenario can come true… or pretty darn close, especially if you take every opportunity to build a relationship with the employer.

Your job search letter may be your first chance to "get personal" with your reader. With the right approach, your letter can catapult you ahead of your competitors. That's what Part 1 is all about—developing a winning job search letter strategy aimed at establishing a special connection.

By the way, don't be surprised if the guidelines in this section pay off when you write other types of letters: business, proposal, press release, and even personal.

Chapter 1

You Gotta Have a Strategy

In This Chapter

➤ Two strategies for writing letters that will jump-start your job search

➤ How employers respond to cover and broadcast letters

➤ Understanding which letter strategy is better for you

Strategy is the magic word behind big success stories: Fortune 500 companies, Olympic champions, life-saving humanitarian efforts, Nobel Prize winners... *your job search!* Your career advancement strategy has many facets, one of which is sending a strong letter.

There are two methods for using job search letters: the cover letter strategy and the broadcast letter strategy. In this chapter, you'll learn about these two tactics and how to choose the ideal one for your situation.

Tip
"There's no security in having a job. Real security comes from knowing how to work the job market."—A saying in the career development field.

What "Flavor" Letter Works for You?

Don't you just love choices? Given too many, some people get Baskin Robbins flashbacks and go on eating binges. Before you charge off to the freezer where you have all 31 flavors, read on. Then if you decide to eat ice cream while you do this project, go ahead!

Deciding which type of job search letter to use isn't nearly as baffling as choosing an ice cream flavor. After all, I'm talking about only *two* choices: a cover letter or a broadcast letter.

Watch Out!
When responding to an ad in the newspaper, use the cover letter and resume method. Most applications are initially screened by human resources departments, and they tend to favor this traditional approach.

The Buddy System

A cover letter is your resume's buddy. It's a brief "sales" letter that enhances your resume so that yours stands out from other resumes on an employer's desk. (Details on how to write a cover letter are in Part 2.)

To get a feel for the cover letter strategy, check out the following cover letter and resume for Carolyn Hyden. Notice how her letter and resume complement each other.

Carolyn Hyden

001 Pacifica St.   •   Atlanta, GA 89602   •   (123) 123-1234

April 20, 199X

Ms. Jody Raas
01 Rue L'Orange
Paris, France

> In both her resume and cover letter, Carolyn refers to her merchandising program.

Dear Ms. Raas,

When I read about your company in *Harpers Bazaar,* I immediately sought out the opportunity to become familiar with your line at the Atlanta Bloomingdale's.

What excites me most about your design is its contemporary presentation of classic lines — a look I believe will appeal to sophisticated Americans, if properly merchandised.

As you can see from my enclosed resume, I helped develop highly successful "Merchandise Coordinator Programs" for Ralph Lauren and Ellen Tracey. In both instances this program dramatically increased sales by giving the designer control over visual presentation.

I am eager to boost your U.S. and/or European sales by using this proven merchandising technique, and am willing to relocate to France, if necessary. I will call your office next week to see when we can arrange a telephone appointment.

I look forward to our conversation.

> Carolyn isn't shy. She initiates the idea of an international telephone appointment. Good call!

Sincerely yours,

Carolyn Hyden

Enclosure: Resume

> This cover letter makes specific reference to Carolyn's enclosed resume.

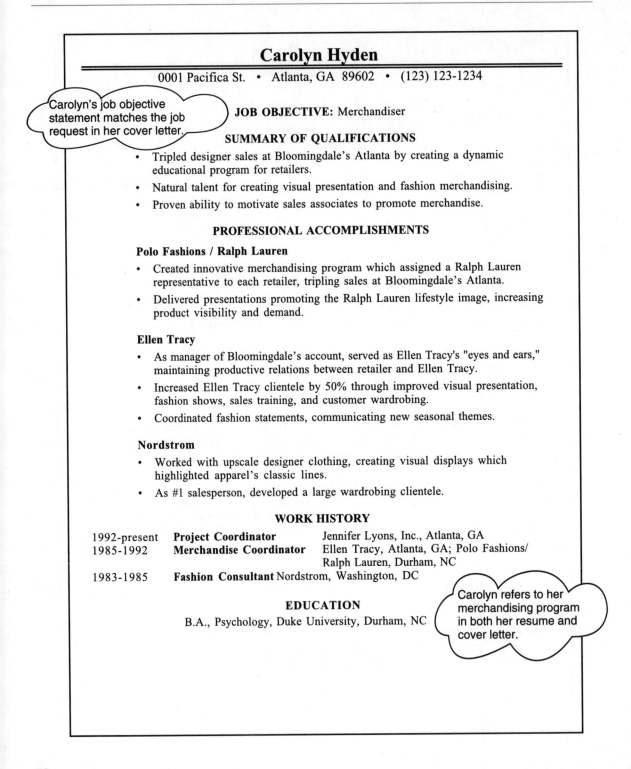

Carolyn Hyden

0001 Pacifica St. • Atlanta, GA 89602 • (123) 123-1234

Carolyn's job objective statement matches the job request in her cover letter.

JOB OBJECTIVE: Merchandiser

SUMMARY OF QUALIFICATIONS

- Tripled designer sales at Bloomingdale's Atlanta by creating a dynamic educational program for retailers.
- Natural talent for creating visual presentation and fashion merchandising.
- Proven ability to motivate sales associates to promote merchandise.

PROFESSIONAL ACCOMPLISHMENTS

Polo Fashions / Ralph Lauren

- Created innovative merchandising program which assigned a Ralph Lauren representative to each retailer, tripling sales at Bloomingdale's Atlanta.
- Delivered presentations promoting the Ralph Lauren lifestyle image, increasing product visibility and demand.

Ellen Tracy

- As manager of Bloomingdale's account, served as Ellen Tracy's "eyes and ears," maintaining productive relations between retailer and Ellen Tracy.
- Increased Ellen Tracy clientele by 50% through improved visual presentation, fashion shows, sales training, and customer wardrobing.
- Coordinated fashion statements, communicating new seasonal themes.

Nordstrom

- Worked with upscale designer clothing, creating visual displays which highlighted apparel's classic lines.
- As #1 salesperson, developed a large wardrobing clientele.

WORK HISTORY

1992-present	**Project Coordinator**	Jennifer Lyons, Inc., Atlanta, GA
1985-1992	**Merchandise Coordinator**	Ellen Tracy, Atlanta, GA; Polo Fashions/ Ralph Lauren, Durham, NC
1983-1985	**Fashion Consultant**	Nordstrom, Washington, DC

Carolyn refers to her merchandising program in both her resume and cover letter.

EDUCATION

B.A., Psychology, Duke University, Durham, NC

Q & A

Which do employers generally read first: the resume or the cover letter?

It's completely up to the employer and, believe it or not, *you*! That's right, you have more control over the reader than perhaps you realize. Your graphic design will make one document look easier to read than the other. Employers want to know as quickly as possible: 1) who you are; 2) what you want; and 3) why you should have it. Therefore, they will reach for whichever piece of paper (letter or resume) delivers that message faster. So use your computer or typing talents to pull your "prospect's" eyes to either your "sales" letter or resume (your choice) by making one look more inviting to read. (Learn more about graphic techniques in Chapter 10.)

Solo Performance

A broadcast letter is exactly what it sounds like—a letter that announces to an employer what position you're looking for and why you're qualified. What makes a broadcast letter different from a cover letter? A cover letter is accompanied by a resume; a broadcast letter does not have a resume enclosed—it gives an award-winning, solo performance.

Simply put, a broadcast letter is a hybrid of a resume and a cover letter. It's a letter sent in lieu of a resume and cover letter. And because a broadcast letter stands on its own, its message needs to be packed with powerful achievements. (More about broadcast letters in Part 4.) The following letter by James Lorrian and the broadcast letters in Chapter 12 will give you an idea of what a broadcast letter looks like. (Notice there is no accompanying resume for this or any broadcast letter.)

Watch Out!

CAUTION

There's a movement afoot in some organizations to totally do away with the use of resume/cover letter packets. These groups tout a philosophy that the only winning marketing piece is the broadcast letter. Don't fall for this narrow approach. Evaluate both techniques (cover letter/resume and broadcast letter) and decide for yourself based on the criteria mentioned in this chapter.

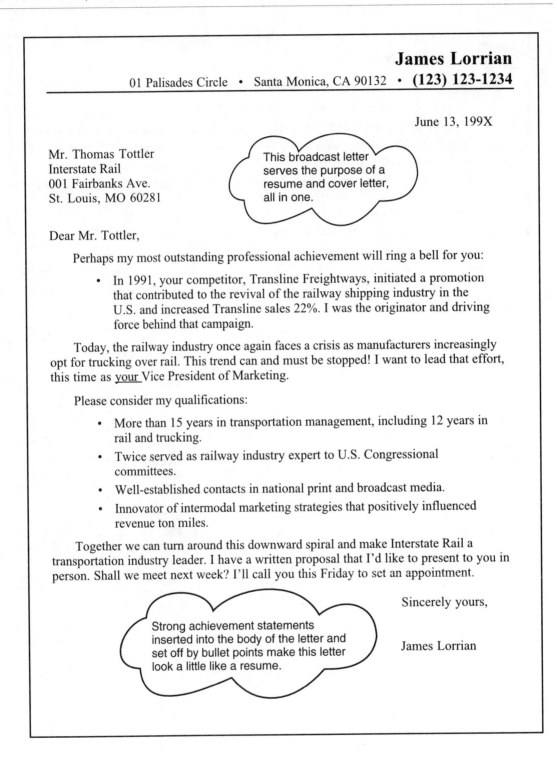

James Lorrian

01 Palisades Circle • Santa Monica, CA 90132 • **(123) 123-1234**

June 13, 199X

Mr. Thomas Tottler
Interstate Rail
001 Fairbanks Ave.
St. Louis, MO 60281

This broadcast letter serves the purpose of a resume and cover letter, all in one.

Dear Mr. Tottler,

Perhaps my most outstanding professional achievement will ring a bell for you:

- In 1991, your competitor, Transline Freightways, initiated a promotion that contributed to the revival of the railway shipping industry in the U.S. and increased Transline sales 22%. I was the originator and driving force behind that campaign.

Today, the railway industry once again faces a crisis as manufacturers increasingly opt for trucking over rail. This trend can and must be stopped! I want to lead that effort, this time as your Vice President of Marketing.

Please consider my qualifications:

- More than 15 years in transportation management, including 12 years in rail and trucking.
- Twice served as railway industry expert to U.S. Congressional committees.
- Well-established contacts in national print and broadcast media.
- Innovator of intermodal marketing strategies that positively influenced revenue ton miles.

Together we can turn around this downward spiral and make Interstate Rail a transportation industry leader. I have a written proposal that I'd like to present to you in person. Shall we meet next week? I'll call you this Friday to set an appointment.

Sincerely yours,

James Lorrian

Strong achievement statements inserted into the body of the letter and set off by bullet points make this letter look a little like a resume.

Q & A

If I send an employer a broadcast letter, will I need to send a resume later on in the application process?

You will very likely need to send a resume. After receiving your knock-out broadcast letter, your future employer will call you for an interview. Whether or not she asks you to bring along a resume, you should have one ready to present at the interview. Your resume will serve as a useful tool for steering the conversation and as accurate notes for your interviewer's files.

Pros and Cons

There's no *one* right letter strategy (cover letter vs. broadcast letter), however, there will be one that is better suited for *your* situation. To choose between the two, you need to weigh the following:

➤ The employer's perspective

➤ Your personal style

To understand the impact of each of these factors, read on...

Looking Through the Employer's Eyes

Let's divide employers into two personality types—conservative and open-minded—and explore how these two types view cover and broadcast letters.

➤ The conservative employer will appreciate a resume and cover letter because it fits into his or her system. This type of employer is probably looking for someone who understands the importance of policy and procedure, and will appreciate your adherence to the tradition of sending a resume. The conservative manager may view a broadcast letter as a gimmick—an attempt to go around procedure in order to get attention. For the conservative reader, I suggest using the resume and cover letter strategy.

Tip
The broadcast letter works especially well in a small-sized company where your letter's chance of reaching the person in charge is greater than in a large company.

➤ To the open-minded manager, your broadcast letter could send just the right message—that you're innovative and you value a personal approach. The fact that you've chosen such a novel form of communication might demonstrate skills desirable on the job. If you feel your prospective employer will applaud an unconventional, creative approach to your application, use the broadcast letter strategy.

Know Thyself

Now let's look at the two types of letter writers—cover letter writers and broadcast letter writers—to figure out which type you are.

➤ The cover letter writer usually prefers a formal approach to reaching his or her goals. For this job seeker, stepping out of the norm (which is what the broadcast letter asks him to do) feels uncomfortably risky. He'd rather follow standard policy (in this case, sending a resume and cover letter) and he does it superbly. He creates a resume and cover letter that makes him stand head and shoulders above his competition. If you identify with this job seeker's personality, use the cover letter and resume strategy.

➤ The broadcast letter writer is naturally creative, tends not to stand by tradition, and loves the excitement of stepping "outside the box" in almost everything he or she does. This job seeker writes a good broadcast letter that makes a powerful statement about her character—she's a confident professional who's willing to break with tradition to be noticed. She's willing to take the chance of seeming like a renegade, knowing that if she wins, she's apt to win big. If you're a risk taker of this kind, consider going with the broadcast letter strategy.

Making Up Your Mind

Which of the two strategies are you going to choose? Here are my thoughts on how to determine the best one for you. Weigh the pros and cons mentioned above, using both your logic and your intuition to come up with the right solution for you.

If you can't decide between the two approaches, read Parts 2 and 4 to get a better feel for how each type of letter works. If, after that, you're still in a quandary, go with the cover letter and resume method. It's the safest approach and no employer will fault you for taking that route.

Now that you've decided which strategy you're going to employ, your next step is to read Chapters 2 and 3 for some important points that apply to both types of letters. Then turn to Part 2 if you're a cover letter writer or to Part 4 if you're a broadcast letter writer for step-by-step instructions for developing your letter.

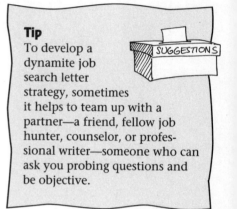

Tip
To develop a dynamite job search letter strategy, sometimes it helps to team up with a partner—a friend, fellow job hunter, counselor, or professional writer—someone who can ask you probing questions and be objective.

The Least You Need to Know

➤ A cover letter is sent to an employer along with the job seeker's resume. It serves as an introduction and states why the job seeker is a good fit with the prospective employer's company.

➤ A broadcast letter is a hybrid of a resume and a cover letter. It is not accompanied by a resume and therefore must, on its own, convince the employer that you deserve a job interview.

➤ The cover letter strategy is best for job seekers who prefer to follow standard protocol and is especially appropriate when applying to a conservative company.

➤ The broadcast letter strategy is for adventurous job seekers who wish to take an innovative approach to their job application. A broadcast letter can make a strong impression on an open-minded employer.

Chapter 2

Winning Concepts

In This Chapter

➤ Use your job search letter to establish a personal connection with an employer

➤ Let your letter exude personality... in an appropriate way

➤ Set the job-offer wheels in motion with compelling phrases

➤ Make sure your letter gets attention by having a good graphic design

Whether you own a new sports car or an old jalopy, a sure way to drive from point A to point B is to jump into your buggy, follow a map, and pay attention to signs along the way. Likewise in your job search, to go from a blank sheet of paper to a polished letter, jump onto your high-speed computer (or drag out your pen and paper) and follow the guidelines in this chapter.

Four Rules of the Road for Writing a Dynamite Job Search Letter

Use the following four "Rules of the Road" as the basis for creating a letter that will stand out—in a positive way, I assure you!—from everyone else's, even in that huge stack of letters on the employer's desk. As you peruse this book, you'll notice these rules distributed like signposts wherever I think you might need some direction.

Tip
Your cover letter may be your first opportunity to show interest, not just in *any* job or *any* employer, but in a *particular* job and a *specific* employer.

Rule #1: Establish a Connection

Rule #2: Show Personality

Rule #3: Initiate Action

Rule #4: Make It Quick and Easy to Read

Now let's look at each one of these rules to understand why they're so important.

Rule 1: Establish a Connection

The Honorable Mayor Richard Daly of Chicago once said, "We don't want nobody, nobody sent!" It always helps to have a name to drop or an inside hitter to push things along.

Using personal contacts is the name of the game. A personal connection in your job search can be of three types:

1. You already know the person you are writing to. (For instance: You met her at a party; you provided a consulting service to her department three months ago; or you introduced her at a local community group meeting last week.)

Watch Out!
Before you blurt out the name of the person who "sent" you, make sure he or she is in good standing with the employer. It won't help you a bit to say that the boss's secretary, Mary, recommends you if Mary just got fired for stealing pencils from the stock room.

2. You know a friend or associate of your addressee. (For example: Your college professor was also his professor; your cousin works in his company; or your neighbor plays bridge with his wife.)

3. You have an affinity with the company, which infers a professional connection with the reader. (For instance: You served on a committee with representatives from the reader's firm; you read an article in last Sunday's paper that featured the company; or you once conducted a survey which concluded the superiority of the company's product.)

Who Do You Know?

Think hard now...what connections do you have, and how can you use them in your letter to make the most convincing presentation? In answering these questions, look for a gold nugget to place at or near the beginning of your first paragraph—a name that will hook an employer into reading your message.

Q & A

Won't it seem contrived to drop names in my cover letter?

Not at all. In fact, your reader will appreciate being able to reference you according to someone he or she knows. The employer will likely figure, "I respect so-and-so (who you mentioned in your letter), so I'll probably like this job seeker." That's the response you want and need!

Samuel Laden's letter on the next page exemplifies how to immediately establish personal contact in a job search letter.

What if you don't have an existing personal connection at your prospective place of employment? Then make a conscious effort to win as many friends as quickly as possible inside the company where you'd like to work. Every time you call the company, introduce yourself to the person on the other end of the line and be sure to catch their name, regardless of where they fall in the company hierarchy. Solicit advice, help, and information from each contact until you've built a solid network of people and resources. Then you can incorporate names appropriately into your job search letter.

Watch Out!
When dropping someone's name in a letter, ask his or her permission to do so, especially if you're saying he or she recommends you for the job.

CAUTION

Notice how Brenda Oppenheim's letter on page 17 establishes a sense of personal contact, even though the only person she knows in the company is a receptionist she spoke with on the phone once.

SAMUEL LADEN

123-123-1234

001 Monk Road
Gladwyne, PA 19035

June 11, 199X

Mr. Joseph Kazinski
Deputy Managing Editor
Philadelphia Inquirer
P.O. Box 20223
Philadelphia, PA 19023

Dear Joe,

In 1981, you helped launch my career in lifestyle reporting and editing by hiring me as a stringer. After that first job, I spent ten years with newspapers in Pennsylvania, including seven with the *Pittsburgh Sun-Times,* before moving to Oklahoma in 1991.

Once again, I'm seeking a position in the Philadelphia area, and would appreciate being considered as a *Philadelphia Inquirer* Lifestyle Section Editor.

I have always had a great deal of respect for the content and layout of the *Inquirer's* lifestyle section, and would love to be part of your team. Having developed a particular expertise in natural health and beauty products, I have a hefty Rolodex of contacts in the field.

I am enclosing my resume, along with some clippings, to show you how my work has matured over the years. I'll call you next week so we can talk more about employment possibilities. Thank you!

Sincerely yours,

Samuel Laden

Enclosure: resume

Speech bubble: Samuel sends a clear message that he's a good candidate for the job.

Speech bubble: In his first line, Samuel tickles his reader's memory of how they know each other.

Speech bubble: Samuel purposefully says he will call his reader.

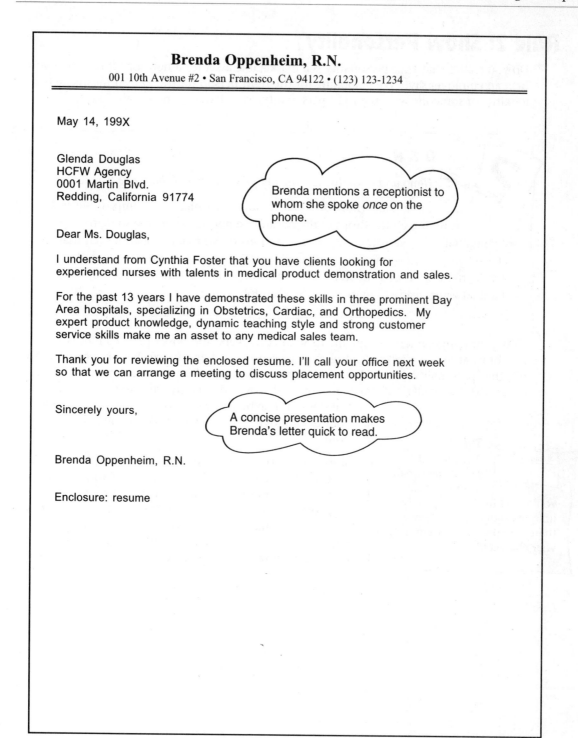

Brenda Oppenheim, R.N.
001 10th Avenue #2 • San Francisco, CA 94122 • (123) 123-1234

May 14, 199X

Glenda Douglas
HCFW Agency
0001 Martin Blvd.
Redding, California 91774

> Brenda mentions a receptionist to whom she spoke *once* on the phone.

Dear Ms. Douglas,

I understand from Cynthia Foster that you have clients looking for experienced nurses with talents in medical product demonstration and sales.

For the past 13 years I have demonstrated these skills in three prominent Bay Area hospitals, specializing in Obstetrics, Cardiac, and Orthopedics. My expert product knowledge, dynamic teaching style and strong customer service skills make me an asset to any medical sales team.

Thank you for reviewing the enclosed resume. I'll call your office next week so that we can arrange a meeting to discuss placement opportunities.

Sincerely yours,

> A concise presentation makes Brenda's letter quick to read.

Brenda Oppenheim, R.N.

Enclosure: resume

Rule 2: Show Personality

Do you realize that your personality is a marketable asset for a new job? It is! When you hear an employer say, "We're looking for the right person for the job," it means he is looking for someone with the right personality, as well as experience and skills.

Q & A

How can I possibly show my full personality in a short, one-page letter?

Revealing your whole personality can sometimes feel as impossible as catching all the drops of the ocean in a bucket. There are so many aspects of your character. Narrow your "ocean" of traits down to a list of about ten that are relevant to the job you want. (A full explanation for creating your personality list is coming right up in this chapter.) That way, you'll have a handy bucketful, instead of a tidal wave, ready to market during your job search.

How your temperament complements your coworkers' and boss's personalities is a big part of what makes a job satisfying. So, in a sense, you have an excellent opportunity to test the "personality waters" by revealing your character through your letter. If your style clicks with the reader's, chances are you've discovered a happy work setting for yourself.

Tip

A letter that reveals personality is one that says you're "selling" a completely unique product—you—since there's no one else with exactly your character!

If it doesn't, maybe you've saved yourself an unhappy bout of employment that would have ended on a sour note.

Since having the right personality could be a key qualifier for the job you seek, think carefully about which of your traits you would like the employer to know about. I suggest that before you start writing your letter, you make a list of your characteristics, even the ones you think might be perceived as negative. Before you make your list in the following worksheet, take a peek at the lists made by Janet, James, and Skip.

Janet	*James*	*Skip*
Organized	Methodical	Driven
Willing	Quiet	Analytical
Hard worker	Logical	Funny
Good follow-through	Exacting	Organized
Articulate	Friendly	Linear thinker
Witty	Team spirited	Tough negotiator
Independent	Patient	Workaholic
A loner	Slow (Oops!)	Rude (Oh no!)
Smart		
Impatient (Uh oh!)		

Ready to make a list of your characteristics? Don't be shy. No one is going to see this list except you, so be honest about both your winning and "losing" traits.

MY PERSONALITY TRAITS

_____

_____

_____

_____

_____

_____

_____

_____

_____

Now that you've compiled a list of your qualities, let's consider how to appropriately inject personality into your letter.

Optimizing the Positive

Once you've decided which of your wonderful qualities you want to show your potential employer, how are you going to let those subtleties come across in your letter? Here are three ways to make a personality statement.

➤ Illustrate your personality by the way you phrase your sentences. For instance:

If you want to show that you're a friendly person, use friendly, chatty language throughout your letter. Stay away from stilted phrases, so that your letter sounds more like a telephone or in-person conversation than a formal document. Check out the congenial tone used in the letter by Peggy Tierazano on the next page.

If you want to show that you're clever, you could use a witty turn of a phrase. This can frequently be done by using the company's slogan, product name, or terminology peculiar to their industry. For an example of this technique, see Charles Bragg's letter on page 22.

To demonstrate humor, say something funny. This is tricky, since a joke can easily fall on its face. But if you're a natural comic, go for it. See Pamela Little's letter in the Appendix.

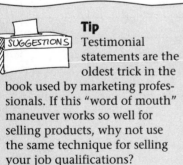

Watch Out!
Revealing your true personality in your letter may screen you out of possible employment. The flip side is that by wearing your heart on your sleeve, you increase your chance of finding true job satisfaction, since you're more likely to get matched with a work environment with values and attitudes similar to yours. I strongly urge you to put all bets on the personality horse that's galloping toward the finishing line marked "job satisfaction."

Tip
Testimonial statements are the oldest trick in the book used by marketing professionals. If this "word of mouth" maneuver works so well for selling products, why not use the same technique for selling your job qualifications?

➤ Say outright that you have a particular quality. For instance, create a sentence like one of the following:

"I resolve customer problems using friendliness, firmness, and negotiating skills."

"My witty marketing style has left its signature on several national advertising campaigns."

"My sense of humor has more than once turned a sour deal into a pot of gold."

➤ Quote someone else who thinks you have a suitable personality. Maybe your boss, coworker, or client has said something noteworthy like:

"We couldn't have made it through five minutes of that grueling trade show without John's humor." — Typical feedback from coworkers

"On our team of five MBAs, Linda's wit led the pack." —Jim Frieberg, Marketing Communications Director

"Thanks to Sherry's diplomacy and sense of humor at a critical juncture, these negotiations went through like a breeze." (Former supervisor)

Peggy A. Tierazano
001 Channon Lane ☆ Lafayette, CA 94549 ☆ 123/123-1234

July 13, 199X

Bill Byham
CEO/President
DDI Pharmaceuticals
001 Bronson Way
Pittsburgh, PA 19187

Peggy's letter draws her reader in with chatty language.

Dear Bill,

How was your trip to Japan? I hope you made it to the plane on time!

I want to thank you for making my "temp job" as your media escort most enjoyable. And when you asked to see my resume, I felt like I'd won the lottery.

As you suggested, I contacted Pam Jensen at your Kansas City office, and had a good chat with her about the opening you'd mentioned. The details she gave me increased my enthusiasm even further.

I also spoke with my husband about the possibility of moving to Pittsburgh, and he welcomed the idea. We are both eager to move back to the East Coast, for the reasons you and I discussed.

As far as I'm concerned, everything sounds like a "go"! How shall we proceed from here? I'll call you next week (after you've had a chance to unpack your bags!) to see what we can set up.

Best,

A little humor helps Peggy end on a memorable note.

Peggy A. Tierazano

Enclosure: resume

Charles L. Bragg

001 Highland Park / San Francisco, CA 94110 / 123/123-1234

September 11, 199X

Mr. George Scoll
President, Marketing Division
Mattel, Inc.
001 Market Street, Ste. 2000
Cincinatti, OH 30321

> Charles cleverly incorporates the name of the company's product, "The Point."

Dear Mr. Scoll,

You've got a point -- The Point, that is. What a dynamite new video game! Kudos to all who were involved in its development. If my 12-year-old's reaction is typical, you've got a potential hit on your hands.

Notice I said "potential." Because, as we both know, having a terrific product is only *part* of the marketing battle. And that's where I come in. As your marketing coordinator, my first goal will be to ensure that our prime market, the five to ten year-olds, get The Point!

You may not recognize my name, but you know my work. Remember the sensation created a few years ago by the Cabbage Patch dolls? I was a key player on the team which launched that product -- to spectacular success!

Then there were the trolls. They were big in the early '60s, then vanished for over twenty years. It was a good buddy of mine, Ralph Keyes at Toys R Us, who brainstormed with me about reintroducing them. I gave him some merchandising "helpful hints" -- and it flew!

In my professional opinion, it's critical to the success of The Point that I get involved now -- before the game has time to languish on the market, or get upstaged by the latest Nintendo. I've got some innovative ideas to run by you. Lunch next week? I'll call you on Friday.

Most cordially yours,

> By speaking of specific products, Charles shows that he knows what's up with this employer.

Charles L. Bragg

Enclosure: resume

Spinning a Negative Into a Positive

Identifying your positive qualities is usually easy. But what about the "negative" ones? (And, by the way, we all have some difficult characteristics.)

Given careful thought, some of your so-called "negative" qualities could be given a positive spin. Take a look at how the three job seekers mentioned earlier in this chapter turned lemons into lemonade.

➤ Janet realizes that she is sometimes impatient because she is a perfectionist. Her drive for perfection is what makes her so precise with details and complex data. Her impatience can be marketed as an "insistence on precision."

Q & A

Time after time I've ended up in jobs I don't like, and which seem to bring out the worst in me. What can I do to stop this pattern?

Your worst personality traits may be emerging because you're not using job skills you enjoy. Before applying for a particular position, be sure its job description requires your preferred skills. And when you write your resume and cover letter, emphasize your favorite skills so that an employer will offer you responsibilities that use those skills.

➤ James is the slowest of all the proofreaders at the publishing house where he works. The big pay-off for the company is that he turns out manuscripts with far fewer errors than his coworkers. Therefore, his slowness can be translated into "accuracy" when he writes his job search letter.

➤ Skip is a collections agent whose secret of success is his ability to intimidate debtors. His terse style may not be an appreciated attribute in some fields, but it leads to an exceptionally high rate of success in getting people to pay their debts. He speaks proudly to prospective employers about his ability to "communicate with clients in no uncertain terms."

Watch Out! CAUTION
Ignorance is not bliss when it comes to recognizing your own pitfalls on the job. Personal awareness of your "faults" can help you determine an appropriate career objective and aid you in marketing your relevant talents.

In the following letter, Wendy makes a dynamite point about how her "negative" quality is going to make big bucks for her next employer:

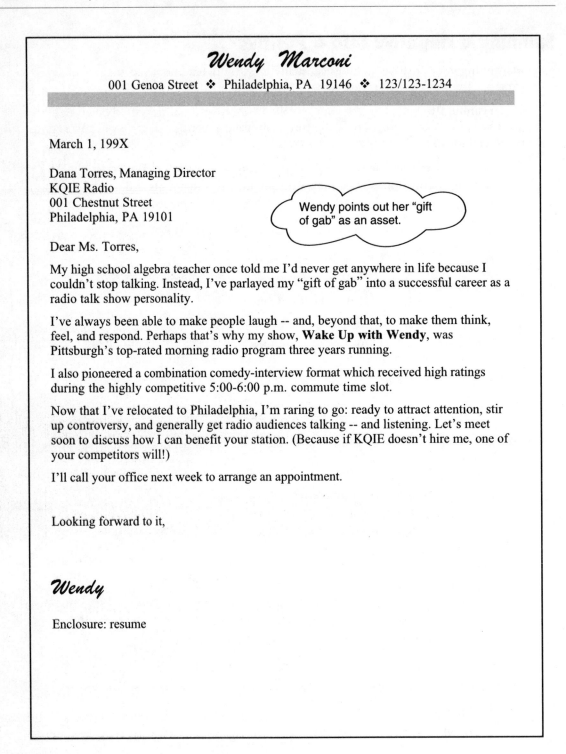

Wendy Marconi

001 Genoa Street ❖ Philadelphia, PA 19146 ❖ 123/123-1234

March 1, 199X

Dana Torres, Managing Director
KQIE Radio
001 Chestnut Street
Philadelphia, PA 19101

> Wendy points out her "gift of gab" as an asset.

Dear Ms. Torres,

My high school algebra teacher once told me I'd never get anywhere in life because I couldn't stop talking. Instead, I've parlayed my "gift of gab" into a successful career as a radio talk show personality.

I've always been able to make people laugh -- and, beyond that, to make them think, feel, and respond. Perhaps that's why my show, **Wake Up with Wendy**, was Pittsburgh's top-rated morning radio program three years running.

I also pioneered a combination comedy-interview format which received high ratings during the highly competitive 5:00-6:00 p.m. commute time slot.

Now that I've relocated to Philadelphia, I'm raring to go: ready to attract attention, stir up controversy, and generally get radio audiences talking -- and listening. Let's meet soon to discuss how I can benefit your station. (Because if KQIE doesn't hire me, one of your competitors will!)

I'll call your office next week to arrange an appointment.

Looking forward to it,

Wendy

Enclosure: resume

Rule 3: Initiate Action

The main purpose of your cover letter is to initiate action. Your whole letter is adding up to one simple climax: to motivate the employer to take the next step toward offering you your new job.

If you're writing a cover or broadcast letter, the activity you want to initiate is probably a telephone or in-person interview. If you're writing a thank-you letter after an interview, your goal is most likely to get called for the second interview or to get a job offer.

A good job search letter includes a push for the next step, which usually appears near the end of the letter with a statement that indicates what *your* next move is (e.g., to call the employer's office, to drop off a portfolio of samples, to come by to set up an interview appointment). Chapter 8, "Step Four—Closing the Sale," outlines how to compose your statement of action.

There are two important questions to keep in mind while creating your letter.

1. What is the action that I want the reader to take as a result of this letter?

2. How can I motivate him or her to take that action?

Make sure your letter answers these questions before signing your name. Notice how Richard Wagner specifically asks for a job interview in his letter, which appears in the Appendix.

Tip
Keep the ball in your court, if at all possible, when you instigate your reader to take action. For instance, in the last paragraph of your letter, you may have done a great job of asking the reader to invite you for an interview—but don't stop there! Motivate him further by writing that you will call him in a few days.

Tip
When an employer first gets your cover letter and resume in hand, you have only *eight seconds* to convince him to read your information in detail. We're talking about a quick scan by a very busy manager! For that reason, it's vital that you format your material so that it's inviting and quick to scan.

Rule 4: Make It Quick and Easy to Read

Because time is such a valuable commodity in today's hectic world, it stands to reason that a letter that takes less time to read is more likely to get read than a lengthy one. Therefore, less is more—more effective at grabbing the reader's attention.

Keep your letter short! That means:

➤ No more than one page

➤ Short paragraphs

➤ Lots of white space on the page

It's All About Sales!

You're writing a sales letter of sorts, so you don't need to tell the whole story—just give the employer enough of a tease to make him or her want to talk to you in person. By distilling points into a minimum of words, you automatically put down only the very best stuff. So even though you provide less information, it's all high quality information, making the letter more impressive.

Q & A

Is it imperative that my cover letter be only one page long?

You've probably heard the expression, "Time is money." No matter how your next employer defines time, you can be sure of one thing: It's valuable to her! For that reason, you'll get brownie points for respecting her time by sending a concise, easy-to-scan letter. And that means a *one-pager*.

Here's how to achieve brevity:

➤ Create a clear list of what you want to say. (More about this in the next chapter.)

➤ Say what's on your list and no more.

➤ Present your material in a one-page format that gives the appearance that a quick scan will tell the reader all he or she needs to know.

Watch Out!

CAUTION

If, despite my advice against it, you decide to have a two-page letter, put "continued" at the bottom of page one, and your name and "page two" at the top of page two so that the two sheets can be rejoined if they get separated.

Hmm, This Looks Interesting!

When you're all done with your letter, "stand back" and ask the question, "What's going to jump out at the reader?" Most probably it will be the first line of the first paragraph (hope it's a grabber!), lists or bullet points you may have inserted in the body of the page (you know, those juicy achievement statements), and any short, short paragraphs (where you threw a powerful one- or two-liner punch). In other words, the elements that pop out should be so hot, they entice the employer to read your master-piece word for word.

Following the Rules

Sometimes the word "rules" makes people shudder, imagining old school days when not following institutional guidelines meant detention or some horrible punishment. Well, not the case in letter writing. These are very loose rules—more like "words from the wise." In fact, the more creative you are in incorporating these principles, the more effective your sales letter will be.

Notice the variety of ways the Rules of the Road show up in the following letter, as well as the sample letters in the Appendix.

Isabella Grimaldi

001 Oak Road ✉ Berkeley, CA 94708 ✉ (123) 123-1234

June 23, 199X

Ms. Kathleen Lincoln, Manager
Gourmet Gallery
001 W. Third Street
Oakland, CA 94611

Establish a Connection: Right in the first line Isabella reminds Kathleen how they know each other.

Dear Kathleen,

When we last spoke at the Gourmet Gallery cooking class, you suggested I submit my resume for part-time employment. I would consider such a position an ideal opportunity for me to share my:

Make It Quick and Easy to Read: Short paragraphs and bullet point statements make this letter a snap to read.

Show Personality: Does Isabella sound excited about cooking, or what?

- Enthusiasm for food preparation;
- Knowledge of culinary tools; and
- Love for bringing people together around delicious cuisine.

In addition, I truly enjoy working with people to find the best solutions for their needs. You'll note in my resume that in many positions I acted as "Co-Chair" or "Co-President" — an appropriate role for me, since I thrive in a team-oriented environment.

Kathleen, I hope we can get together soon to talk more about this possibility. I'll follow up with you next week, if I don't hear from you before then. Thank you!

Sincerely,

Initiate Action: You bet! In the last paragraph Isabella "threatens" to call Kathleen if Kathleen doesn't call her first.

Isabella Grimaldi

Enclosure: resume

The Least You Need to Know

➤ Establish a personal connection with the reader of your letter as quickly as possible.

➤ Give the employer a sense of your personality through your writing style, direct statements about your character, or testimonial references.

➤ Understand what you would like the employer to do as a result of your letter—and motivate him or her to do it.

➤ Format your one-page letter using short paragraphs, bullet points, and white space to make your communication look quick and easy to read.

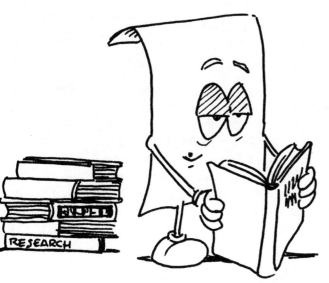

Research Smarts

In This Chapter

➤ Learn how to create a letter that speaks directly to the employer's concerns

➤ Make your letter sound personable by developing a profile of the hiring person

➤ Prepare to write a concise and powerful letter by compiling a list of points you want to make

Knowing what makes your prospective employer tick will help you clarify why you want to work for her, and will enable you to articulate those reasons convincingly. Since your letter is intended to say you're a good fit for the company in question, it makes sense that you frame your experience and qualifications in terms of the company's business goals, products, etc. To achieve that effect, you need to research, research, research!

In this chapter, you'll learn about two important areas of research and how to combine the results of your investigations into a concise list of what your job search letter needs to convey.

Q & A

What if I don't have time to conduct my job hunt research?

Hire someone to do it for you. Surprised? Don't be. There are people who will do research to your specifications for a price. A good professional researcher will use on-line capabilities, libraries, and the good ol' telephone to dig up more stuff than an archeologist. Where do you find such a research animal? Ask a career counselor to suggest one, look in your Yellow Pages under "career," "jobs," "employment," "researchers" or some such title; or call the career center of a local college and ferret out an ambitious student needing a little extra cash in return for her brains, time, and hard work.

What's the Company Up To?

Use every resource you can think of to educate yourself about your prospective employer's history, market standing, goals, challenges, mission statement, industry, clientele, corporate culture, etc. Good places to seek this information include:

➤ Business sections of public and school libraries where you'll find references like: *Dun & Bradstreet's Million Dollar Directory*, *Thomas' Register of American Manufacturers*, and *Standard and Poor's Register of Corporations*

➤ Business and financial magazines such as *Fortune, Forbes Magazine,* and *Upside*

➤ Business sections of newspapers

➤ Your prospective employer's company literature (You can ask the company to send you brochures, annual reports, catalogs, and the like.)

In addition to these sources, consider who in your personal and professional networks might know anything about the company. Maybe your Uncle Eddie used to work in the firm and still has contacts there. Someone in your career development support group might be a former employee of the company. Your career counselor might have valuable insight. Scour your Rolodex to see if you know anyone who might have relevant information.

Q & A

What does it mean to "network" for a job?

Say the term *job networking* and picture a carefully crafted net (like a fishing net) with you (the job hunter) in the center reaping the benefits of all that falls into your net. Made of invisible "threads" that extend from you to all the people you know, to the people those people know, and so on, your "net" work becomes a conduit for ideas, favors, and information for your job search. With a strong network, you could be the recipient of a big job search pay-off!

Who's Who?

Your next task is to identify the hiring manager for the position you want. You may find his or her name in company literature, from an inside company contact you've developed, or as the result of a cold call to human resources.

A company with a human resources department usually wants applications to go through that department (after all, that's why the department was created). But ultimately, the one who will make the hiring decision will be the supervisor for the job you seek. That's the person you want to address in your letter, even if the letter goes through human resources initially. (More about this procedure in Chapter 4, "The Power of a Cover Letter.")

Pulling It All Together

Compile your company information into a format something like the following. (Of course the contents of your format depends on what information you're able to glean.)

COMPANY PROFILE

Company's name: Westwood Running Shoes

Company's location: Los Angeles, California

Company's principle product: Running shoes

Company's other products: Socks, T-shirts, shoe laces, sports decals

Hiring manager for department I'm interested in: Mr. Alfred Jones, VP of Marketing

Company's annual revenue: $14 million

Customer demographics: 43% ages 18 and under, 35% ages 19-30, 17% ages 30-45, 5% ages 46 and over

Projected growth: $28 million in three years

continues

Chief competitor: Anchor Line Shoes

Company promotional slogan: Westwoods, for those in the fast lane

Product endorsement: Marathon champion, Fred Williams

If it's absolutely impossible for you to gather information about the company you're applying to (let's say you're responding to a classified ad in the newspaper that doesn't reveal the company name), here's what I suggest: Create a speculative profile of the company in question, using your best guesses and whatever industry knowledge you have.

Here's an example of what I mean.

SPECULATIVE COMPANY PROFILE

Company's name: Unknown

Company's location: Los Angeles area, California

Company's principle product: Running shoes

Company's other products: Probably socks, T-shirts, shoe laces, sports decals

Hiring manager for department I'm interested in: The head of the marketing department

Company's annual revenue: Most likely $10-14 million

Customer demographics for industry: 43% ages 18 and under, 35% ages 19-30, 17% ages 30-45, 5% ages 46 and over

#1 Company in industry: Anchor Line Shoes

Ready to create a company profile for your job search? Here you go...

COMPANY PROFILE

Company's name:

_____

_____

Company's location:

_____

_____

Company's principle product or service:

_____

_____

Company's other products or services:

_____

_____

Hiring manager for department I'm interested in:

_____

_____

Annual revenue of company:

_____

_____

Customer demographics for company or industry:

_____

_____

#1 competition in industry:

_____

_____

Other useful information about the company:

_____

_____

_____

_____

_____

Getting to Know You

OK, you've got the name of the person to whom you're addressing your letter. Now you need to find out as much as possible about him. You want to get a sense of his personality, management style, hiring preferences, work ethics, and maybe something in his history that relates to yours (e.g.; you and he went to the same prep school; he belongs to the same church you do; you both pilot planes).

Now, how are you going to find this stuff out? You have to put on your Sherlock Holmes hat and start investigating your subject. (Of course, use discretion in how you conduct your research. You don't want your prospective employer to feel that he's being stalked.)

Tip
Developing a hiring manager's profile will help you write a letter with a personal tone. This profile will drive home the fact that you are writing to a living, breathing *person* (someone with a personality, achievements he's proud of, and maybe interests you share), not an inanimate object.

Watch Out!
Never cross the fine line between questioning and badgering when you hunt down information about your prospective employer. Be sensitive to how people respond to your queries and recognize when you've started to wear out your welcome. If they seem uneasy with your probing, it's time for you to turn to another source or drop the matter altogether. There's no point in annoying the very folks you hope to be associated with in your next job.

Rule
Rule #1: Establish a Connection. While conducting your Scotland Yard investigation, you're likely to develop some contacts that you can mention in your letter. So, jot down your informers' names for future reference. (More about name dropping in Chapter 6, "Step Two—Follow My Lead.")

Here are some ideas for getting the scoop:

➤ Ask members of your network what they know about the manager.

➤ Search the literature you've collected to find articles your prospective boss might have written.

➤ Spend some time at your library checking Who's Who books and local newspapers on microfilm to find articles written by or about your potential employer. Many libraries have CD-ROM databases where you can search names in print.

➤ If you're on-line savvy (or looking for an excuse to become familiar with the Information Superhighway), conduct a World Wide Web search by company name, industry, and CEO or manager's name. Many companies and individuals have their own sites where you get a lot of information.

➤ Call local organizations (such as the Chamber of Commerce, professional associations, community organizations) that you think your prospective employer might belong to. Maybe he's scheduled to give a talk or lead a meeting that you could attend.

See what I'm saying? Think of ways to learn as much as possible about your addressee before writing him a letter. That way, you can write about issues that will spark his interest. (In Chapter 7, "Step Three—The Pitch," you'll learn how to compose sentences to address your reader's concerns.)

As you gather information, create a hiring manager's profile, something like this:

HIRING MANAGER'S PROFILE

Name: Mr. Alfred Jones

Title: Vice President of Marketing

Company: Westwood Running Shoes

Age: 47

How long with company: 4 years

Promotions within company: None. He was hired straight into VP position

Number of people in his department: He directly supervises five, indirectly 27

Reports to: CEO and CFO directly

Articles or talks: Published one article in *International Marketing Magazine*, April, '96 entitled "Fast pace marketing for running shoes."

Anything relevant to me: This man ran the Boston Marathon the same year I did, 1987. We're both avid sports enthusiasts—love competition.

Other information: Someone at my job support group said Jones is a super friendly guy, but a tough negotiator. That tells me to be extra sharp when it comes to salary negotiations.

Q & A

I'm not comfortable introducing myself to strangers. How can I overcome my insecurity about doing this important part of my research?

I'm sure that at least once in your life you've felt good about "rescuing" a complete stranger by giving him or her directions or explaining something. Now the shoe is on the other foot—you're going to make someone else feel good about giving you a hand with your project. Most people like to meet and help other people. To ease your nerves, first jot down the one or two questions you want to ask. Then, take a few deep breaths, put on a winning smile, pick up the phone or open the door, and say something like: "Hello! My name is so-and-so. Could I ask you a few questions about your company?" Each time you repeat the experience, you'll do better. You're going to do just fine!

What if you try to investigate the hiring manager and all your leads go nowhere? Don't despair! You can still build a profile that, despite the possibility that it won't be absolutely accurate, will give you the psychological advantage of knowing your addressee is a real person (not a faceless corporate entity). In other words, based on what you know about the company, imagine what the manager *might* be like and create a speculative profile like this:

Rule
Rule #2: Show Personality. Do you realize how much easier it's going to be to reveal your character once you have a sense of your reader's personality? That's a good reason to develop the manager's profile.

RULES OF THE ROAD

SPECULATIVE HIRING MANAGER'S PROFILE

Name: Mr. Alfred Jones

Title: Vice President of Marketing

Company: Westwood Running Shoes

Age: Probably in his 40s

How long with company: I think more than two years and less than seven

Number of people in his department: Enough to handle marketing in 37 states and three European countries

Reports to: At his level, most likely to CEO and CFO

Articles or talks: Don't know, but I'll bet he's articulate and represents his company to professional organizations one way or another.

Anything relevant to me: I'm going to guess this is a man who thrives on competition. He probably has a family and is interested in wholesome living, e.g., sports, running, outdoor stuff—all things I like.

Other information: For the sake of developing a mental image of Mr. Jones, I can picture him wearing a suit to the office, having a confident business manner, and easily slipping into a track suit and running shoes after work.

Now it's your turn. Use the following worksheet to come up with a manager's profile for your job search.

HIRING MANAGER'S PROFILE

Manager's name:

_____

_____

Manager's title:

_____

_____

Company name:

_____

_____

Manager's age:

_____

_____

How long he or she has been with company:

_____

_____

Number of people in his or her department:

_____

_____

Manager reports to whom:

_____

_____

Articles or talks he or she has written or been featured in:

_____

_____

Any of his or her history, activities, or interests common to me:

_____

_____

Other information:

_____

_____

_____

_____

_____

Making a List and Checking It Twice

Here's the most important part of your strategy: determining what you want to say in your letter. Now remember, you're not going to be writing a long epistle—just a short sales letter with three or four main points.

So, based on the information you have about the company and the hiring manager (refer to the profiles you just made), develop a list of items you want to incorporate into your letter. In your list, make sure to include the following points:

1. What position you'd like. (This could be the exact job title you're applying for or a brief description of the role you'd like to play in the reader's organization.)

Q & A

How do I ask for a particular position, if I don't know what I want?

A strong career strategy and some good research should help you clarify and articulate your job objective. Your career strategy will tell you what role you want to play for an employer and what skills you want to highlight in that position. Your research will tell you what job title requires the skills you love to use. If you can't figure out what the exact job title is, you can use a generic statement such as, "a management position with a focus on finance."

Watch Out!
Don't be lazy! Uncovering or creating a personal connection may seem like a lot of work, but believe me, it's worth it! It could mean the difference between your letter getting noticed or thrown away.

2. Your link to the organization or to the reader personally. (Your link could be how you learned about the job opening; someone you know at the company; or something you and the reader have in common that supports your job objective.)

3. Why you're a good fit for the organization. (Maybe you have a particular skill they're looking for; you're aligned with the company mission statement; or you're familiar with their product since you used to sell it in your last job.)

Q & A

Do employers really care about "soft" stuff like my personal philosophy?

Some employers do, especially if your philosophy lines up with the organization's mission. After all, if you share the values and goals of the company where you work, you'll be a more dedicated employee.

4. What you'd like to accomplish with this letter. (The result you probably seek is to get an interview.)

Your "to-say" list can be as simple as one of the following:

SALLY'S "TO-SAY" LIST

1. Say I want to be Accounting Manager.
2. Tell the employer I know her best friend.
3. Explain that I have always had the same professional philosophy as the company's mission statement.
4. Ask for the interview.

TOM'S "TO-SAY" LIST

1. Announce that I would like to be their customer service representative.
2. Let the reader know I have a really effective approach to customer service that will solve her problem.
3. Name two achievements to convince her I know what I'm talking about.
4. Request an interview.

FRANK'S "TO-SAY" LIST

1. Say I'm after the graphic designer opening in their marketing department.
2. Mention that I won the same art contest he did at the same art school.
3. List two achievements that say I'm qualified.
4. Offer to bring in my portfolio and stay for an interview.

Let's take a peek at how Sally's list panned out into an effective cover letter.

(Let's check that Sally made all four points on her "To-Say" list.)

Sally Winship
01 Dogwood Avenue
Beverly Hills, CA 90532
(123) 123-1234

February 9, 199X

("Tell the employer I know her best friend." Dianne Pilsner (mentioned in the first line) is Louise's best friend.)

Ms. Louise Walker, CFO
Westwood Running Shoes, Inc.
01 West Oakcaster Rd.
Los Angeles, CA 90128

("Explain I have the same philosophy as the company mission statement." There it is in the first paragraph!)

Dear Ms. Walker,

My former co-worker, Dianne Pilsner, and I have spent countless lunch hours talking about where Long Laces, Inc. could have gone on Wall Street if it had had a mission statement similar to Westwood's. I've always admired Westwood's bold marketing style and innovative business approach.

Recently Dianne called me with the news that you have a management opening in your Accounting Department. After 15 successful years as Accounting Manager for two smaller companies, I'm eager for a change to a company of Westwood's stature.

I will call you next Tuesday to see when we can meet to talk about the Accounting Manager position. Meanwhile, I'll enclose my resume for your review. Thank you.

Sincerely yours,

("Say I want to become Accounting Manager." Sally achieves that in paragraph #3.)

Sally Winship

("Ask for an interview." Sally uses her last paragraph to say she wants an interview.)

Enclosure: resume

Here's a worksheet for your "to say" list.

TO SAY IN MY LETTER

1. What position I'd like.

_____

_____

2. What link I have to the organization or to the reader personally.

_____

_____

3. Why I'm a good fit for the organization.

_____

_____

4. What I'd like to accomplish with this letter.

_____

_____

At this point, don't worry about how to say these things in your letter. I'm going to cover that in Parts 2 and 3. For now, just create a list of what items you want to say.

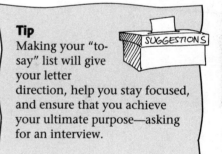

Tip
Making your "to-say" list will give your letter direction, help you stay focused, and ensure that you achieve your ultimate purpose—asking for an interview.

Now What?

Now that you know WHO you're writing to and WHAT you want to tell her about yourself, it's time for the fun part: composing the letter itself! In the next two parts, you'll see just how to do that.

The Least You Need to Know

> ➤ Research is a key factor in creating a successful letter—learn as much as possible about your reader's company.
> ➤ Find out who will make the hiring decision for the job you want and address your letter to that person.

➤ Investigate the hiring manager to learn about his or her personality, concerns, management style, and any interests you may have in common.

➤ Compile your research in charts called "company profile" and "hiring manager profile."

➤ Make a list of points you want to cover in your letter including the name of the position you want, why you're qualified for the job, and a request for an interview.

Part 2
Your Resume Booster

If you feel "Overwhelmed" with a capital "O" as you sit down to write your cover letter, you're not alone. That's how most job seekers feel when they set out to impart the "I want the job" message to the "almighty" employer.

You realize, of course, that one of the reasons writing your letter seems so daunting is because it's a promotional piece about you (no offense intended). Think about it: If you were writing a letter about someone else or, better yet, a product such as a new candy bar, it would be infinitely easier. You'd be more detached and therefore, the subject matter would be greatly simplified. As it is, you know so darn much about yourself, it's hard to imagine picking out what's most marketable and putting it down in only three or four short paragraphs.

Well, I've got the solution. I've broken the process into four straightforward steps. That way, you don't have to figure it all out at once—you can take it one step at a time.

First, sit down at your desk in front of your computer or at your kitchen table with a paper and pencil. Close your eyes, take a deep breath, and imagine that I'm sitting right at your elbow. Then open your eyes, turn the page, and let me guide you through the whole thing—from typing your name at the top to signing your name at the bottom.

The Power of a Cover Letter

Sometimes the simplest request, like "Please send a resume and cover letter," can be enough to send you into a tailspin. "Why a cover letter?" you want to scream back. "It took me five days to write my last one and it still wasn't that good. What's the point of a cover letter anyway? Isn't my resume enough?"

That's a common reaction among job hunters. In this chapter, I'm going to explain how sending a good cover letter along with your resume can enhance your candidacy for a job. Understanding what a cover letter can do will help you write one that works powerfully for you.

The Big Deal About Cover Letters

It's very tempting to just fold up your resume, stuff it in an envelope, and send it solo to a prospective employer, isn't it? Don't do it! You worked hard to create a dynamite resume that effectively highlights your strengths and skills. Don't let all that hard work go to waste—ensure your resume's success by introducing it with an equally strong letter.

Here are five reasons for sending a cover letter along with your resume.

1. You'll increase your chances of grabbing the employer's attention.
2. Your letter can highlight aspects of your resume.
3. It gives you a chance to start what could be "the best conversation of your career."
4. Your letter is probably your first opportunity to make a personable impression.
5. You can directly ask for a job interview.

Sound intriguing? Good. Let's look at each one of these advantages, one at a time.

Get Noticed

Surveys show that resumes with cover letters (no matter how bad those letters are) get more attention from employers than resumes without cover letters. Even a poorly written cover letter shows an attempt to make personal contact with the hiring manager. Imagine how effective a stimulating letter will be!

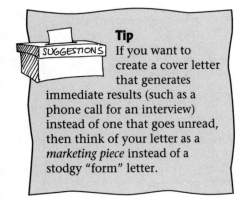

Tip
If you want to create a cover letter that generates immediate results (such as a phone call for an interview) instead of one that goes unread, then think of your letter as a *marketing piece* instead of a stodgy "form" letter.

Your resume and cover letter are akin to valuable real estate—yes, high-priced downtown property where every increment of space can explode into profitability if used wisely. This "real estate" (those sheets of paper you're going to stuff into an envelope and ship off to your prospective employer) has the potential to pay you big dividends—both in terms of salary and job satisfaction. Since you are using two documents in your marketing packet—the resume and the cover letter—the cover letter represents 50% of your marketing real estate. Wow, that's a lot of power for a short letter, and a big piece in your strategy to win the job of your dreams.

So, don't waste half of your marketing force by writing a crummy cover letter. Write one that really sends a whammy to your next employer.

The Perfect Resume Marriage

Your letter can highlight or elaborate on significant aspects of your resume. You've already produced a tight, punchy resume that zings with accomplishments. (If not, you need to read my book, *The Complete Idiot's Guide to the Perfect Resume.*) In your resume, there may be a particular achievement that you want the employer to be sure to read. If so, use your cover letter as a spotlight and shine it on that glowing statement. If the achievement is a total knockout, talk about it a little in your letter, being sure to make connections to the potential employer's situation and needs.

Check out Cindy White's letter on the next page and John Kreiger's in the Appendix to see how these job seekers used their cover letters to accent accomplishments in their resumes.

⌘---Cindy White--- ⌘
001 Precita Avenue, #2
San Francisco, CA 94110
⌘--- 123/123-1234--- ⌘

February 22, 199X

Ms. Jana Thompson
Starlight Alaska Cruises, Inc.
001 North Seventh Street
Mill Valley, CA 94030

Here's an immediate declaration of Cindy's job objective.

Dear Ms. Thompson,

Your search for "an experienced sales manager with proven results in group and incentive sales" has stimulated my application for the position.

I offer over 10 years' experience consistently meeting -- and frequently exceeding! -- management's passenger and revenue goals for FIT and group bookings.

The enclosed resume details my extensive background in cruise industry sales and marketing, coupled with an in-depth knowledge of area travel agencies and leisure markets.

I'll call your office next week so we can talk more about how my abilities could benefit your firm. Thank you for your consideration.

Sincerely,

Cindy wrote a strong assertive close.

Cindy's achievements are hard for an employer to overlook!

Cindy White

Enclosure: resume

Rule

Rule #1: Establish a Connection. Just as most conversations start with some sort of ice breaker, your letter can serve as an ice breaker by bringing up something or someone you and your potential employer have in common. Once the ice is broken, you're ready to talk business!

Rule

Rule #2: Show Personality. Imagine the employer picking up your letter and asking himself, "Who is this person and how will she fit into my club?" So in addition to stating your skills and experience, drop hints about what kind of person you are. Are you likely to become the department organizer, the motivator who leads the team to defy all former sales records, or the ultimate champion of overtime endurance?

The Start of a Beautiful Relationship

You can use your letter to mention a special connection you have to the company (you know someone there, you've used their product all your life, your father invented one of the machines they use in manufacturing, etc.). I'm going to talk more about how to create a link with your reader in Chapter 6, "Step Two—Follow My Lead." For now, suffice it to say that your letter is an excellent opportunity to start a "conversation" with your reader, a conversation you hope will continue for years to come.

Your Winning Personality

Because your cover letter is conversational by nature, it's an outstanding chance to show that you have the right personality for the job. Of course, during your job interview, the hiring manager is going to be checking out your personality. But before you even get to the interview, you need to make the best impression possible.

Get the Job Done

In your cover letter, you can pointedly ask for the next step: an interview. Yep, you're going to out-and-out ask for a job interview (and in Chapter 8, "Step Four—Closing the Sale," I tell you how to pop the question in a way that ensures you get an answer). Your resume on its own doesn't "press" the reader to grant you a chance at winning her over in an interview. Your cover letter does!

Here's what this all boils down to: You really *do* need a cover letter, even when you have a powerful resume.

Q & A

Aside from job applications, I use cover letters for non-job search projects such as business plans, school applications, and consulting proposals. Do the same principles apply in such cases?

Most definitely yes. Your letter still complements your accompanying documents in the same five ways mentioned above.

Carry an Umbrella So It Won't Rain

My mother used to say, "Better carry an umbrella so it won't rain." I guess her advice was kind of a twist on Murphy's law: *"If you don't have an umbrella, it will definitely rain."* I'm passing my mother's tip on to you, this time with regard to your resume and cover letter. Whether you're the kind of person who generally takes extra precautions or not, here's an occasion where I suggest you plan for the worst, and hopefully it won't happen.

It's quite possible that your resume and cover letter will get separated at some point during the shuffle, after it reaches the address on your envelope. Can you imagine? After all the work you've done to pair these two marketing pieces (your resume and cover letter), they might get split up? Unfortunately, that's the nature of paperwork, especially in large firms.

Watch Out!
"If there's a way for your cover letter to get separated from your resume during the application process, it will."—Murphy's Law for job hunters

Cover Your Bases

Just in case Murphy's Law is in full force when your letter and resume arrive in Ms. Employer's hands, your job search will still succeed if you do the following:

1. Create a resume that works beautifully with a cover letter but also stands strongly on its own. One way to achieve that is to be sure that your resume has a job objective statement on it and therefore isn't dependent on your cover letter for that message. The other is to customize your resume for the specific job at the company you are applying to.

2. Write a cover letter that is such a knockout it can "sell" you, even without a resume. That way, if your letter refers to an enclosed resume, the employer will call you up, confess that your resume has gotten lost, and ask you to send another directly to his attention because he absolutely must see it.

If you do both numbers 1 and 2, you'll have your bases covered if the two pieces of paper get separated. Imagine how power-packed your presentation will be if they end up staying together!

Notice how the next cover letter and resume by Joshua Alis complement each other, yet can stand alone as strong marketing pieces.

JOSHUA M. ALIS
189 Lakeview Avenue • Ringwood, NJ 07456 • (800) 001-1111

February 12, 199X

Joshua's letter refers to his resume without summarizing it. Good move!

Mr. Bob Stippel
Ciba Animal Health
2122 Woodstream
Kingwood, TX 77339

A play on words with the name of the company's product shows that Joshua is witty.

Dear Mr. Stippel,

In the process of talking with Dr. Howard Hesby of A&M University, I learned about your new venture, The Program. I know a dynamite product when I hear it, and I want to be one of the first sales managers to get with "The Program."

The enclosed resume highlights some of my accomplishments in the animal health industry over the last six years. My educational sales approach has proven so successful that numerous manufacturers, distributors, and sales representatives now look to me as an expert in the animal health industry. Needless to say, this reputation opens many doors and business opportunities.

Thank you for taking the time to consider my qualifications. I will call your office in a few days to learn when we can talk in person. In the meantime, please feel free to contact me at 1-800-001-1111.

Sincerely yours,

His confident close demonstrates that Joshua knows how to win a sale.

Josh Alis

Enclosure: resume

Matching letterhead makes Joshua's resume and cover letter a graphic match.

JOSHUA M. ALIS
189 Lakeview Avenue • Ringwood, NJ 07456 • (800) 001-1111

JOB OBJECTIVE: Sales/Buying Consultant in the animal health industry

SUMMARY OF QUALIFICATIONS
- Six years' experience with leading animal health/agricultural companies.
- Consistently exceed sales goals by thinking and working "outside the box."
- Extensive network of key industry contacts.

PROFESSIONAL ACHIEVEMENTS

1994-present   STRAIGHT ARROW PRODUCTS, Bethlehem, PA
Manufacturer of Mane 'n Tail equine and human grooming products.
Regional Manager — New York, New Jersey, and Pennsylvania

- Produced news story aired on ABC-TV and throughout Asia, boosting domestic and international visibility.
- Expanded sales by 45% YTD, working with over 65 sales reps to develop Gold Key and prospect accounts.
- Increased individual sales 900% by creating and presenting "Prescription for Success," a three-hour demonstration.
- Created new markets through beauty supply wholesalers, marketing equine products for human use.
- Penetrated the beauty salon market by securing an account with a top department store's in-house salons.

1991-94   AMERICAN CYANAMID COMPANY, Nebraska Area
A leader in animal nutrition industry, selling feed grade antibiotics/biologics.
Field Sales Representative, 1992-94

- Increased sales 152% in one year through strong consultative approach.
- Expanded strategic regional account 25-fold by promoting increased profit margin and market share, as well as valuable sales and technical support.

Telesales Representative (TSR), 1991-92

- Tripled personal average sale through pro-active telesales techniques.
- First TSR to reach $750K in annual sales (company norm: $400K).

EDUCATION
B.S., Animal Science — Industry Option (GPA in major: 3.1), 1989
Texas A&M University, College Station, TX

Specific achievements support Joshua's job objective.

A concise job objective makes this resume work independent of Joshua's cover letter.

53

Going Through Human Resources... or Not

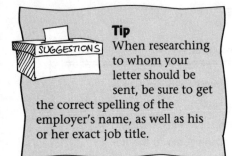

Tip
When researching to whom your letter should be sent, be sure to get the correct spelling of the employer's name, as well as his or her exact job title.

When sending your resume and cover letter to a company, find out to whom you should address your packet. In some firms, you will be asked to send it directly to the hiring manager.

Large companies frequently have a human resources department (also referred to as "HR") to handle initial job search inquiries, screen applicants, and process personnel records. Since the company has devised the HR system to expedite the hiring process, it makes sense to use or at least acknowledge its HR department. Read on to see what I mean by "use or at least acknowledge" HR.

Go Straight to the Top

Rule
Rule #1: Establish a Connection. By writing directly to the manager in charge of your hoped-for position, you take a bureaucratic link out of your job search chain, bringing you that much closer to forming a personal relationship with your "new boss."

Your goal in sending your resume and cover letter is to reach the hiring person, one way or another. If you know the name of that manager, I suggest you send it directly to him or her. If, however, you don't know their name, but know the name of the department where you would like to work, you could address your letter to the director of the department (e.g., Director of Marketing, Sales Manager, Director of Production).

"cc" You Later

In either case (sending it to the exact hiring manager or to the director of the department where you would like to work), I suggest that you make the following diplomatic move:

1. Put "cc: Human Resources Department" at the bottom of the letter you have addressed to the hiring manager or department director. (See an example of this technique in Andrew Wilmington's letter in the Appendix.)

2. Send a copy of the letter (addressed to the hiring manager with the "cc" at the bottom) and resume to the human resources department.

Q & A

Isn't "cc" an outdated term, since hardly anyone uses carbon paper anymore?

Although the term *cc* (which stands for "carbon copy") was originated before the invention of computers and copying machines, we still use it today to mean "copy of this document sent to."

A "cc" at the bottom of your letter signals both HR and the manager that you have covered all the application bases, and that you honor the HR system the company put in place. In this way, you don't step on anybody's toes, and also save the company some internal copying and distribution work.

Dear Ms. HR

An alternative to writing to the hiring manager is to address and send your letter only to the human resources department and go through the normal (and frequently longer) personnel channels.

Patricia Tower's letter in the Appendix is a good example of how to direct a cover letter to the Director of Human Resources.

Tip

If you choose to send your letter to the human resources department initially, try to find the name of someone in that department to whom the letter can be personally directed. If you can't get a specific name, address your letter to "Director of Human Resources" and say "Dear Director" in your salutation.

Q & A

When a job announcement says, "Include salary history with resume," what should I do?

I recommend that you avoid mentioning your exact salary figures until you're at the interview and can discuss it in person. But in order to comply with the ad's salary history request and get past the initial screening process, include a brief sentence in your cover letter, referring to your salary. See Chapter 9, "Sticky Situations," to learn how to address the salary issue appropriately.

The Least You Need to Know

➤ Sending a dynamite cover letter with your resume adds a personal touch that increases the chances of your resume being read by employers.

➤ A good cover letter strategy is one that works even if the letter and resume get separated.

➤ If possible, address and send your cover letter and resume to the hiring manager, and forward copies of both documents to the human resources department.

➤ Although it's not the most direct route, it's perfectly acceptable to send your letter and resume to human resources.

Step One— Set the Stage

In This Chapter

➤ Design a letterhead that makes your name stand out

➤ Use your address to create a stable image

➤ Present appropriate contact info so an employer calls you

➤ Tips on choosing between four letter formats

➤ How to write your letter's salutation

Before a word of your letter gets read, its graphic appearance is bound to make an impression. Score a home run on this count by using a crisp, professional format that presents your name and contact information in a memorable, easy-to-read way.

As you might have guessed, this chapter is about choosing a format, creating the heading for your letter (sometimes referred to as "letterhead,") and starting your letter with the date, inside address, and salutation.

Q & A

What is "letterhead"?

Letterhead means the section at the top of your stationery that contains your name, address, and contact numbers (phone, fax, e-mail). Read on to learn how you can create a handsome job search packet by using the same letterhead for your cover letter and resume.

To the Letterhead

Have fun designing your letterhead. There are lots of possibilities for type style, positioning of information, and graphic elements such as lines, bullet points, etc. Let your graphics demonstrate your taste and personality (for instance: classy, playful, conservative, trendy, high-tech). Browse through the sample letters in this book and see if any of the letterheads strike your fancy. By the way, I have a full discussion about choosing paper, fonts, and all that fun stuff in Chapter 10, "Wrap It Up."

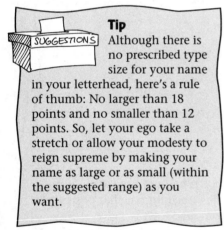

Tip

Although there is no prescribed type size for your name in your letterhead, here's a rule of thumb: No larger than 18 points and no smaller than 12 points. So, let your ego take a stretch or allow your modesty to reign supreme by making your name as large or as small (within the suggested range) as you want.

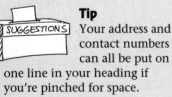

Tip

Your address and contact numbers can all be put on one line in your heading if you're pinched for space.

My Name Is...

Arrange the graphic layout of your heading so that your name appears either in the middle or on the right-hand side of the page. (It doesn't matter how you line up your address and contact numbers.) Here's why: Once your letter is read, it will probably be filed (hopefully in a filing cabinet and not the "circular file.") Because the left-hand side of the paper is usually placed in the spine of a file folder, your name will be seen more easily if you put it either at the top-middle or upper-right corner of the page.

If you think the reader might not be able to tell if you are male or female from your name, decide whether you want him to know. For instance:

Francis Harris (a woman) knows that, although sex discrimination is illegal in the job placement process, the nonprofit organization where she wants to work gives most of its senior management positions to women. Therefore, she wants the reader of her letter to know right off that she is a woman, since it might give her an advantage over the male candidates in the stack of resumes.

Francis has the following options at her disposal in order to clarify her gender on paper:

➤ Use a gender-specific nickname instead of her given name (for example, "Fran Harris" instead of "Francis Harris").

➤ Include a middle name if it's clearly female (for example, "Francis Mary Harris").

➤ Start her name with Ms. (for example, "Ms. Francis Harris").

Think twice before making use of this last option; its formality looks somewhat awkward. However, if you are applying within the U.S. and have an unusual or non-American name that probably won't be recognized as male or female no matter what you do to it, this technique can work.

Now let's look at a situation where it might *not* be to the job hunter's advantage if his sex was known. A man named Robin Hoover is after the same job that Francis (above) wants. In order to get considered for the executive director position, he chooses not to add anything to his name, knowing that his name will keep the reader guessing about his gender—until the interview, of course. At that point, he'll be able to sell himself as a fully qualified candidate.

I Don't Live in a P.O. Box

It's preferable to put your street address in your heading instead of a P.O. box number, since a home address conjures up a more stable image. If, however, you have a specific reason not to give out your street address, it's OK to use a post office address.

Contact Me

You want to be contacted by the employer, don't you? Of course you do—that's the whole point of your letter! So, you need to present the appropriate contact information in your letterhead. There are three types of contact information (aside from your mailing address) that you may wish to list: phone, fax, and e-mail. Let's talk about them.

Rule
Rule #1: Establish a Connection. Contrary to what you may think, your cover letter is not a formal document—it's a marketing piece that serves to introduce you. So, refer to yourself the way you like to be addressed. If your first name is Elizabeth, but everyone calls you Beth, feel free to use "Beth" in your letterhead. Middle initials are optional.

Rule
Rule #3: Initiate Action. One way to encourage an employer to call you for an interview is to make your phone number easy to read. Make the size of the numbers large enough so that from a standing position and without squinting or putting on a special set of glasses, one can read the phone number on your letterhead when it is lying on a desk or table.

➤ Phone

If you list only one phone number in your heading, it will be assumed that it's your home or personal line. If you give more than one phone number, you need to indicate the difference between them. For instance:

Home: 510-555-4238

Office: 510-555-1725

➤ Fax

Fax numbers are not usually found in letterheads since employers seldom fax a response to an applicant. However, when sending your letter to a recruiter, include your fax number (if you have one) in your letterhead since many recruiters fax job listings to job seekers.

CAUTION **Watch Out!**
Don't list your work number in your letterhead unless you can talk freely from that phone and a message can be left without jeopardizing your present job. Never assume that a caller will be discreet on your behalf.

➤ E-mail

Your e-mail address, on the other hand, may be useful. Providing your on-line address could do two things:

1. Expedite the employer's response.
2. Demonstrate that you're on-line savvy (a plus when applying for some positions).

The following two letters point out the variations of letterheads discussed above.

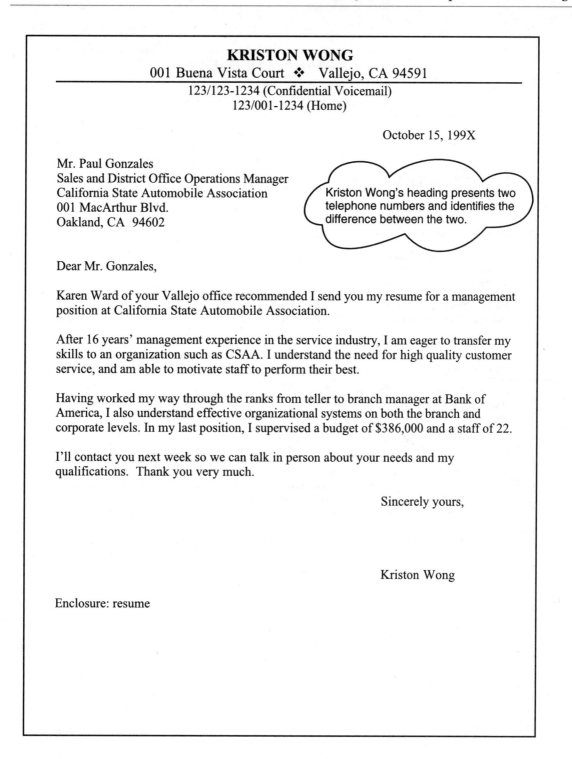

KRISTON WONG

001 Buena Vista Court ❖ Vallejo, CA 94591

123/123-1234 (Confidential Voicemail)
123/001-1234 (Home)

October 15, 199X

Mr. Paul Gonzales
Sales and District Office Operations Manager
California State Automobile Association
001 MacArthur Blvd.
Oakland, CA 94602

> Kriston Wong's heading presents two telephone numbers and identifies the difference between the two.

Dear Mr. Gonzales,

Karen Ward of your Vallejo office recommended I send you my resume for a management position at California State Automobile Association.

After 16 years' management experience in the service industry, I am eager to transfer my skills to an organization such as CSAA. I understand the need for high quality customer service, and am able to motivate staff to perform their best.

Having worked my way through the ranks from teller to branch manager at Bank of America, I also understand effective organizational systems on both the branch and corporate levels. In my last position, I supervised a budget of $386,000 and a staff of 22.

I'll contact you next week so we can talk in person about your needs and my qualifications. Thank you very much.

Sincerely yours,

Kriston Wong

Enclosure: resume

YVONNE MANRIQUEZ

001 E. 14th Street, Oakland, CA 94610

123/123-1234 Ymanriquez@penrap.edu

October 19, 199X

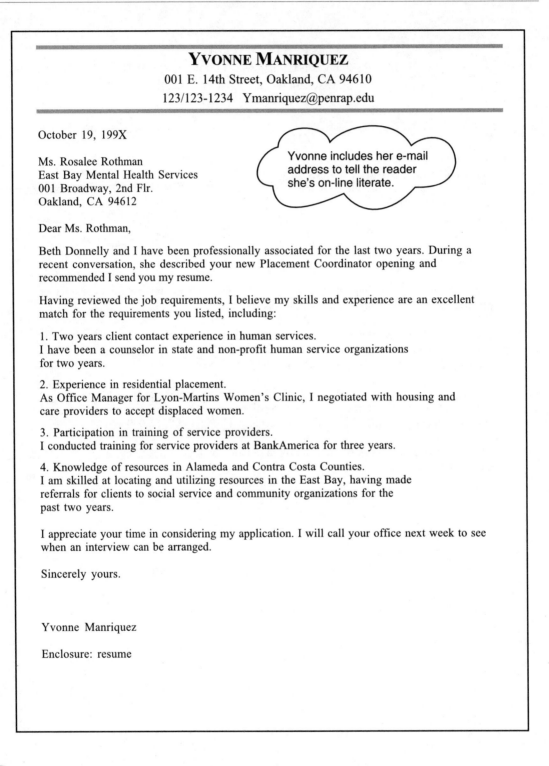

Yvonne includes her e-mail address to tell the reader she's on-line literate.

Ms. Rosalee Rothman
East Bay Mental Health Services
001 Broadway, 2nd Flr.
Oakland, CA 94612

Dear Ms. Rothman,

Beth Donnelly and I have been professionally associated for the last two years. During a recent conversation, she described your new Placement Coordinator opening and recommended I send you my resume.

Having reviewed the job requirements, I believe my skills and experience are an excellent match for the requirements you listed, including:

1. Two years client contact experience in human services.
I have been a counselor in state and non-profit human service organizations for two years.

2. Experience in residential placement.
As Office Manager for Lyon-Martins Women's Clinic, I negotiated with housing and care providers to accept displaced women.

3. Participation in training of service providers.
I conducted training for service providers at BankAmerica for three years.

4. Knowledge of resources in Alameda and Contra Costa Counties.
I am skilled at locating and utilizing resources in the East Bay, having made referrals for clients to social service and community organizations for the past two years.

I appreciate your time in considering my application. I will call your office next week to see when an interview can be arranged.

Sincerely yours.

Yvonne Manriquez

Enclosure: resume

Format Matters

A number of different graphic formats are used in the world of letter writing. Some that work well for job search letters are the block, semiblock, full block, and simplified styles. The following templates demonstrate what these styles look like.

Around the Block Format

This is probably the most popular style. In the block format:

➤ All lines except the date and complimentary close start on the left margin of the sheet.

➤ The date and complimentary close are indented to the far right.

➤ The first line of each paragraph is not indented.

➤ "Enclosure" begins at the left margin.

Q & A

I get confused about the "inside address." Whose address is it, and where does it go?

The *inside address* appears just below the date and on the left margin of your letter. It consists of the addressee's name, job title, company name, and address.

Sorta, Kinda, Semiblock Format

This is a widely accepted style. In this format:

➤ The date is indented to the far right.

➤ Each line of the inside address and the salutation starts on the left margin.

➤ The first line of each paragraph is indented five to ten spaces.

➤ The complimentary close is indented to the far right.

➤ "Enclosure" begins at the left margin.

Q & A

What's the "salutation"? It sounds like something shouted by a pantaloon-wearing guy blowing a horn.

The *salutation* is the greeting used to start your letter. It appears immediately after the inside address. The most common salutation is "Dear so-and-so."

What a Deal: The Full Block Format

This is the most frequently used style for business. In this format:

➤ The date, inside address, and salutation start on the left margin.

➤ The first line of each paragraph in the body of the letter is not indented.

➤ The complimentary close and "enclosure" are on the left.

Q & A

What the heck's a "complimentary close"?

Complimentary close is the closing message on your letter, right before your signature. Just as ham radio buffs say "over and out" right before they sign off, letter writers use a complimentary close like "Sincerely yours."

What Could Be Simpler Than the Simplified Format?

This format is good for cover and broadcast letters that are used for mass mailings. In this format:

➤ The date and inside address start on the left margin.

➤ A subject line appears instead of a salutation.

➤ The first line of each paragraph in the body of the letter is not indented.

➤ The complimentary close is omitted.

➤ "Enclosure" is on the left.

(Block Format Template)

Your name
Street address
City, state, and zip
Contact number(s)

Today's date

Your addressee's name
Professional title
Organization name
Mailing address
City, state and zip

Dear Mr. (or Ms.) last name,

Start your letter with a grabber — a statement that establishes a connection with your reader, a probing question, or a quotable quote. Briefly name the job you are applying for.

The mid-section of your letter should be one or two short paragraphs that make relevant points about your qualifications. You should not summarize your resume! You may incorporate a column or bullet point format here.

Your last paragraph should initiate action by explaining what you will do next (e.g., call the employer), or asking the reader to take a specific step (e.g., contact you to set up an interview). This is also a good place to thank the reader for his or her attention.

Sincerely yours,

Your Name (signed)
Your name (typed)

Enclosure: resume

For an example of the BLOCK FORMAT,
see Melissa Judd's letter in the Appendix for Cover Letters.

(Semiblock Format Template)

Your name
Street address
City, state, and zip
Contact number(s)

Today's date

Your addressee's name
Professional title
Organization name
Mailing address
City, state and zip

Dear Mr. (or Ms.) last name,

Start your letter with a grabber — a statement that establishes a connection with your reader, a probing question, or a quotable quote. Briefly name the job you are applying for.

The mid-section of your letter should be one or two short paragraphs that make relevant points about your qualifications. You should not summarize your resume! You may incorporate a column or bullet point format here.

Your last paragraph should initiate action by explaining what you will do next (e.g., call the employer), or asking the reader to take a specific step (e.g., contact you to set up an interview). This is also a good place to thank the reader for his or her attention.

Sincerely yours,

Your Name (signed)
Your name (typed)

Enclosure: resume

For an example of the SEMIBLOCK FORMAT,
see Connie George's letter in the Appendix for Cover Letters.

(Full Block Format Template)

Your name
Street address
City, state, and zip
Contact number(s)

Today's date

Your addressee's name
Professional title
Organization name
Mailing address
City, state and zip

Dear Mr. (or Ms.) last name,

Start your letter with a grabber — a statement that establishes a connection with your reader, a probing question, or a quotable quote. Briefly name the job you are applying for.

The mid-section of your letter should be one or two short paragraphs that make relevant points about your qualifications. You should <u>not</u> summarize your resume! You may incorporate a column or bullet point format here.

Your last paragraph should initiate action by explaining what <u>you</u> will do next (e.g., call the employer), or asking the reader to take a specific step (e.g., contact you to set up an interview). This is also a good place to thank the reader for his or her attention.

Sincerely yours,

Your Name (signed)
Your name (typed)

Enclosure: resume

For an example of the FULL BLOCK FORMAT,
see Jennifer Freed's letter in the Appendix for Cover Letters.

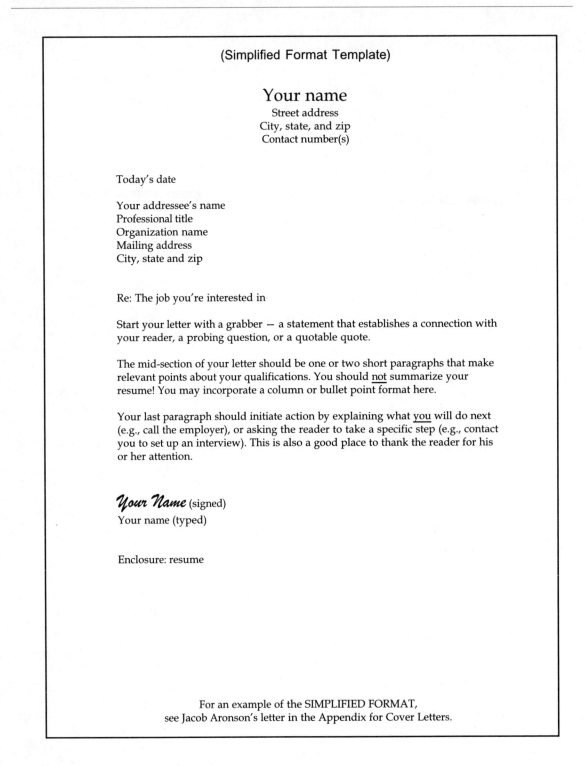

(Simplified Format Template)

Your name
Street address
City, state, and zip
Contact number(s)

Today's date

Your addressee's name
Professional title
Organization name
Mailing address
City, state and zip

Re: The job you're interested in

Start your letter with a grabber — a statement that establishes a connection with your reader, a probing question, or a quotable quote.

The mid-section of your letter should be one or two short paragraphs that make relevant points about your qualifications. You should <u>not</u> summarize your resume! You may incorporate a column or bullet point format here.

Your last paragraph should initiate action by explaining what <u>you</u> will do next (e.g., call the employer), or asking the reader to take a specific step (e.g., contact you to set up an interview). This is also a good place to thank the reader for his or her attention.

Your Name (signed)
Your name (typed)

Enclosure: resume

For an example of the SIMPLIFIED FORMAT,
see Jacob Aronson's letter in the Appendix for Cover Letters.

Make an Executive Decision

What's the right format for you? It's really a matter of personal preference. With the exception of the simplified format, there is no significant advantage of one over the other. The simplified format is far less personal since it doesn't have a salutation or complimentary close. The simplified style is an ideal format for a letter used for a mass mailing. (See Chapter 12, "Announcing, Announcing: Broadcast Letters.")

When and Where

According to which format you use, place today's date in the appropriate place on your computer document or sheet of paper. (See the templates that appear earlier in this chapter to see where the date goes for the format you have chosen.)

You've done your employer research (see Chapter 3, "Research Smarts"), so you know the exact spelling of your addressee's name, his title, company name, and address. This information goes in the spot labeled "inside address" on the template you have chosen.

Rule

Rule #4: Make It Quick and Easy to Read. To identify the format that's best for you, you may need to try out two or three of the styles mentioned here. See which one makes your information the quickest and easiest to read.

There are two ways to position the hiring manager's title in the inside address: either next to the person's name or on the line immediately below his or her name. Either of the following two presentations is correct:

Sharon Smith, Director of Marketing
Fairchild & Sons
1212 Grant Avenue
Kingston, NY 14823

Sharon Smith
Director of Marketing
Fairchild & Sons
1212 Grant Avenue
Kingston, NY 14823

Greetings and Salutations!

The most common way to preface the body of a letter is to put "Dear so-and-so" immediately under the inside address. "Dear" is a safe entrance, even if you have only the job title (not the exact name) of the hiring manager, in which case you could write: "Dear Director" or something of that nature.

Knowing when to say "Dear Sally" and when to say "Dear Ms. Jones" can sometimes be a close call. If speaking on a first name basis is appropriate (based on former contact with the person or how you were introduced), go for it. After all, you do want to further your personal connection with this manager. If, however, you have *any* question that it might seem presumptuous on your part to use his or her first name, don't do it. Resort to Mr. so-and-so or Ms. so-and-so.

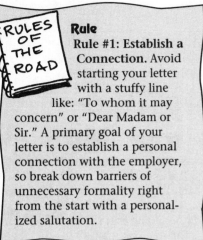

Rule

Rule #1: Establish a Connection. Avoid starting your letter with a stuffy line like: "To whom it may concern" or "Dear Madam or Sir." A primary goal of your letter is to establish a personal connection with the employer, so break down barriers of unnecessary formality right from the start with a personalized salutation.

On rare occasions I eliminate the salutation section and replace it with an announcement like: "Regarding: Position 134765, Assistant Level III." This sterile approach works for government and large institutional jobs where personal connection seems like a near impossibility. By the way, this method is used in the simplified format and sometimes comes in handy for mass mailings.

As you browse through the sample letters in this book, notice some of the creative salutations such as:

Greetings!

Congratulations!

Seasons Greetings!

Q & A

What type of punctuation should I put after my letter's salutation "Dear Ms. Jones"?

For most letters with a friendly, yet professional tone, use a comma after the person's name in the salutation. For more formal letters, it is acceptable to use a colon after the recipient's name.

The Least You Need to Know

➤ When creating your letterhead, place your name in the center or on the right-hand side of the page.

➤ Use the name you would like the interviewer to use when addressing you in conversation.

➤ Create a stable image by providing a street address instead of a P.O. box number.

➤ Include only those phone numbers where employers can leave messages and where you can speak freely.

➤ Include your e-mail address if you think it will impress your potential employer or be relevant to the job.

➤ Use one of the four standard formats for letters, as shown in the templates in this chapter.

➤ The most common and acceptable salutation is "Dear so-and-so"; however you may wish to make a particular impression on the reader by using a more creative entrée.

Chapter 6

Step Two— Follow My Lead

In This Chapter

➤ Grab the reader with your first paragraph... and don't let go

➤ Set the tone for the whole letter right from the get-go

➤ Why the lead sentence of your letter is *so* important

➤ Five types of lead lines

➤ Attention-snatching lead phrases to get you going

Job hunting is kind of like going fishing. (Now this is starting to sound like fun, huh?) You need tasty bait on the end of a fishing line to catch a big fish. The big fish in your job search is the employer of your dreams. And your cover letter "bait" is your first sentence.

This chapter is going to help you reel the big fella in with a great opening paragraph in your cover letter.

What's It All About?

Your first paragraph should be short—just two or three sentences. Its purpose is to rope the reader with a personal contact or phrase that acts like a magnet to keep his eyes going to the next paragraph.

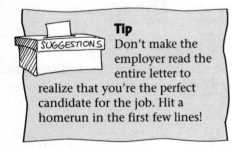

Tip

Don't make the employer read the entire letter to realize that you're the perfect candidate for the job. Hit a homerun in the first few lines!

Rule

Rule #2: Show Personality. Right from the start of your letter, give the hiring manager a sense of your communication style. This is one way for the employer to know how you'll fit into his team.

In addition to grabbing the reader's attention, the *lead paragraph* sets the tone for the rest of the letter (and hopefully the tone of your relationship with your new boss). Assess the company and employer profiles that you created in Chapter 3, "Research Smarts," as well as the list of your personality traits from Chapter 2, "Winning Concepts." Then decide what tone (for instance: highly professional, conservative, compassionate, trendy, humorous, or studious) you wish to put forth in your letter; and use language that lets that quality ring out.

A Well Baited Line

"Great," you say, "I understand that I'm supposed to set the place on fire with my lead paragraph, but how the heck do I do that?" Good question, and one that I have five answers for—just choose one!

1. Mention the name of your personal contact— someone your reader knows.

2. Spring a question that pushes one of the reader's hot buttons and pulls him or her into your train of thought.

Q & A

I'm not comfortable "pulling rabbits out of hats" to get attention. Does that mean I can't write an effective cover letter?

Not at all. Each of the openers listed in this section can be adjusted to your comfort level, whether your style is deeply traditional, or wild and wacky. If you prefer a less dramatic approach, use subtlety when applying the ideas in this chapter to create a letter that is both comfortable for you and effective for your audience.

3. Deliver a bold claim that makes the employer want to know how you could fulfill such a promise, or find out what you're talking about.

4. Start with a quote that snags the reader's attention.

5. Begin conservatively, but in a way which makes a connection between you and the reader (or the company for whom he or she works).

Let's take a look at each of these methods.

Name Dropping

Since name dropping is the name of the game, you could slip the name of the reader's associate or friend into your first paragraph. For example:

> *Blaine Powell recommended I speak with you about your opening for Sales Manager.*

> *My former associate, Ellen Fairbanks, spoke so highly of Tannen & Associates that I decided to send you my resume.*

> *At a recent dinner party, Arthur Lewis told me the inspiring story of his mentorship with you.*

Merl Reinsworth's letter in the Appendix and Larry Hilton's letter on the next page show techniques for capitalizing on a personal connection in the opening sentence.

Rule
Rule #1: Establish a Connection. Name dropping is a sure way to grab an employer's attention, since the person you mention is most likely someone whose opinion your reader trusts (you hope). And by referencing his buddy, you increase the chance of your letter getting read. (If nothing else, the employer will pay attention because he won't want to get caught with his pants down if his colleague asks him about your application.)

Larry Hilton
123/123-1234

001 Bellingham Way
Seattle, WA 98203

April 2, 199X

Ms. Ginny Toland
Director, Human Resources
Southshore Community College
0001 Southshore Way
Bellevue, WA 97903

In his lead sentence, Larry drops the name of a mutual friend.

Dear Ms. Toland,

My good friend Jean Roberts, a history instructor at Southshore, recommended I contact you about your current opening for a teacher of English Composition.

In addition to the traditional qualifications for the post (M.A. in English, coupled with 4 years' teaching experience), my most recent career offers two additional elements which I believe will be valuable to Southshore students:

- Business experience: Having been employed by several large corporations, I have inside knowledge of writing skills necessary for success in the fields of customer service, advertising and sales.

- International experience: During my time with IBM, I worked in China and Japan. This enhanced my understanding of how to teach English writing skills to non-native speakers, as well as my ability to work with a multicultural population.

I will contact you next week to see when we can talk about Southshore's needs. Teaching is my first love, and I am eager to return to it -- and to share with your students my "real-world" knowledge of the business community.

Thank you.

Sincerely,

In his second paragraph, Larry indicates that he is making a career change.

Larry Hilton

Enclosure: resume

Spring the Big Question

Couch your opening phrase in the form of a question. This is tricky to pull off, since you don't want it to sound contrived. You want to stimulate a conversation with your prospective employer by opening a topic of common interest without sounding overly clever or "salesy."

Depending on your reader's personality, position in the company, and industry (all items you included in your company and hiring manager profiles from Chapter 3), determine what kind of question is appropriate to start your letter. In other words, a letter from a database manager to a marketing manager of a multimedia company could start with a splashy lead question like: "When was the last time you had a chance to play Monkey Hijack for fun like your customers do?" On the other hand, a more professional-sounding question like "How long does it take for your marketing data to download?" might be more appropriate for a letter going to a marketing professional in the newspaper industry.

Check out Brenda Brenner's letter, following, and Paul Seifert's letter in the Appendix to see examples of catchy lead-in questions.

Brenda Brenner

001 Chestnut Street, Apt. 102
Philadelphia, PA 19147
123/123-1234

May 1, 199X

Tom Jenks
Director, Human Resources
Focus Camera Corporation
001 Oakdale Street
Philadelphia, PA 19106

Brenda challenges the employer with a thought-provoking question in her opening sentence.

Dear Mr. Jenks,

What would happen if 100% of your customers received excellent, prompt, personalized service -- *without* first spending 5-10 minutes on hold?

As a Focus camera owner myself, I would venture to say that the technical assistance I've received via your 800-number has not been on a par with the products you sell. Please don't take offense; I know your people work hard. But I suspect the right management could dramatically improve their performance -- and that's where I come in!

I am an experienced Customer Relations manager with the know-how to:

- Dramatically improve department efficiency.
- Boost job satisfaction and reduce absenteeism.
- Develop comprehensive, cost-effective training programs.
- Implement quality-assurance systems which ensure results.

After a brief employment hiatus to take charge of some family business, I'm more than ready to re-dedicate myself to what I do best. And, because I believe in your products, I want to do it at Focus.

I will call you next week so we can arrange a time to meet. Thank you.

Sincerely,

Brenda speaks with dignity about her recent stint of unemployment.

Brenda Brenner

Enclosure: resume

Wake Up Call

Launch your letter with a bold opener—usually a very short phrase that demands attention like:

> *Great article in the Sunday paper!*

> *No home appliance store in New York should be without the Wilmington blender!*

> *Franklin Insurance has come too far in the last five years to be missing the Oklahoma market!*

Of course, such a daring starter needs to be followed by a sentence which convinces the reader your letter is worth reading—and not just an empty gimmick. For instance:

> *Great article in the Sunday paper! As soon as I read it, I knew I needed to get my resume to you right away.*

> *No home appliance store in New York should be without the Wilmington blender! I'm ready to make sure each dealer has one.*

> *Franklin Insurance has come too far in the last five years to be missing the Oklahoma market! If you had someone like me in that state, you'd have a huge segment of the marketshare in your pocket.*

In the following letter by Dan Gage and in Lynn Powell's letter in the Appendix, you'll find splashy lead paragraphs.

Watch Out! CAUTION
Don't sound corny or canned with your opening remark. The point is to engage the hiring manager—make her sit up straight and think, "Ah, here's someone who has something to say!" If you can elicit that kind of response, you've already got her wanting to meet you.

Dan Gage
001 Dulcimer Way • Oakland, CA 94602 • (123) 123-1234

January 25, 199X

Human Resources Office
Clara County Community College
001 Mateo Drive
Clara, CA 93403

Dan's opening remark makes the reader sit up straight and nod in agreement.

Dear Human Resources Officer,

Many people say that college students these days have no respect for history, no understanding of the forces which continue to shape world events.

Those people haven't been in my classroom!

I'm a seasoned history instructor, committed to making my subject both *relevant* and *accessible* to students from diverse academic and socioeconomic backgrounds -- in other words, the students at Clara County.

My resume documents my seven years' teaching experiences. I've got a stack of glowing student evaluations I can show you, when we meet. But the qualification that means the most to me is the one I can't put onto paper -- the one you'll grasp only when you watch me in front of a class.

You see, I believe that the study of history is essential to *all* students, even those on vocational tracks. So I've developed innovative teaching methods that spark students' interest... arouse their curiousity... engender their participation... and make them *want* to learn, read, think and write.

Please give me the chance to introduce this approach to Clara County students. Thank you for accepting my application. I will follow up by phone soon.

Yours truly,

Dan talks about his interpersonal talents—the ones that make him such a good instructor!

Dan Gage

Enclosures: Application form, resume, transcripts, list of additional references.

Quotable Quotes

If you know of a quote that speaks to the reader's desire to succeed or articulates a career aspiration of yours, consider starting your letter with that utterance. It could be a famous saying, a not-so-famous saying from a famous person, or just a great comment from an unknown person.

In case your "quotable quotes" memory is a little short, see if one of the following suits your purpose:

Some men see things as they are and ask why. Others dream things that never were and ask why not.

George Bernard Shaw—playwright

There are always opportunities through which business-men can profit handsomely if they will only recognize and seize them.

Paul Getty—founder, Getty Oil Company

Successful men follow the same advice they prescribe for others.

Author unknown

My work is a game, a very serious game.

M.C. Escher—artist

Inform all the troops that communications have completely broken down.

Ashleigh Brilliant—author of quotations

People can have the Model T in any color—so long as it's black.

Henry Ford—founder, Ford Motor Company

The most important persuasion tool you have in your entire arsenal is integrity.

Zig Ziglar—motivational speaker

The price of greatness is responsibility.

Sir Winston Churchill—former British Prime Minister

Leadership is the art of getting someone else to do something you want done because he wants to do it.

Dwight D. Eisenhower—former President of the United States

Everything comes to him who hustles while he waits.

Henry Ford—founder, Ford Motor Company

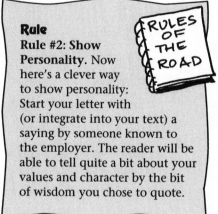

Rule

Rule #2: Show Personality. Now here's a clever way to show personality: Start your letter with (or integrate into your text) a saying by someone known to the employer. The reader will be able to tell quite a bit about your values and character by the bit of wisdom you chose to quote.

Failure is only the opportunity to begin again more intelligently.

Henry Ford—founder, Ford Motor Company

Whether you think you can or think you can't—you are right.

Henry Ford—founder, Ford Motor Company

Let us never negotiate out of fear, but let us never fear to negotiate.

John F. Kennedy—former President of the United States

Nearly all men can stand adversity, but if you want to test a man's character, give him power.

Abraham Lincoln—former President of the United States

What kills a skunk is the publicity it gives itself.

Abraham Lincoln—former President of the United States

Always bear in mind that your own resolution to succeed is more important than any other one thing.

Abraham Lincoln—former President of the United States

The quality of a person's life is in direct proportion to their commitment to excellence.

Vince Lombardi—football coach

You cannot shake hands with a clenched fist.

Golda Meir—former Prime Minister of Israel

There is a real magic in enthusiasm. It spells the difference between mediocrity and accomplishment.

Norman Vincent Peale—Methodist minister and author

Every problem has in it the seeds of its own solution. If you don't have any problems, you don't get any seeds.

Norman Vincent Peale—Methodist minister and author

> **Watch Out!**
> CAUTION
> Understand the meaning of any quote you put in your letter, and know enough about the person you are quoting to be able to have an intelligent conversation about him or her during your interview.

Far and away the best prize that life offers is the chance to work hard at work worth doing.

Theodore Roosevelt—former President of the United States

The buck stops here.

Harry S. Truman—former President of the United States

Failure to prepare is preparing to fail.

John Wooden—college basketball coach

The following letter by Sandy Jones employs the quotable quote technique.

Sandy Elizabeth Jones, l.c.s.w.

001 Florida Street   Berkeley, CA 94601   123/123-1234

April 12, 199X

> The "L.C.S.W." after Sandy's name in the heading tells the reader that she is a social worker.

Betty Kaminsky, Counseling Director
Pacific Center for Personal Growth
001 Telegraph Avenue, Ste. 3000
Oakland, CA 94611

> Sandy aligns herself with a great thinker as a way of stating her own work philosophy.

Dear Betty,

"Every problem has in it the seeds of its own solution. If you don't have any problems, you don't get any seeds." -- Norman Vincent Peale

This quote has always struck me as particularly meaningful to our work in the mental health field. The problems our clients present sometimes seem insurmountable. Yet, we both know of remarkable success stories -- cases where clients turned their lives around. Pam, for instance. She'd spent more than 12 years on the street and on crack, yet I attended her 3-year N.A. "birthday" just last month.

I miss helping some of the community's most challenging clients to plant -- and sow -- those seeds. Despite the rewards of my private practice, I feel a need to do more work "in the trenches" once again. Would there be a place for me (half or three-quarter time) at the Pacific Center?

I'll call you next week so we can set a lunch date. It will be wonderful to see you again!!

Best,

> A case scenario makes Sandy's passion for counseling believable.

Sandy Jones

Enclosure: resume

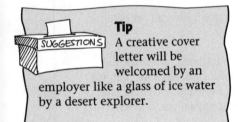

Watch Out!
Don't (I repeat: *don't*) start with a hackneyed line (such as "I am responding to your ad...," "I would like to apply for...," "Enclosed, please find my resume...") that sounds like all the other cover letters in the world. You want to make an introduction that is uniquely yours, and doesn't sound like it's from an automaton.

Tip
A creative cover letter will be welcomed by an employer like a glass of ice water by a desert explorer.

Mind Your Manners

If none of the previous methods are comfortable for you (not everyone finds them appropriate for their personality or situation), use a more conservative entrance that makes a connection between you and your reader.

My resume documents that I have the background and skills to meet your firm's needs for an Associate Research Analyst.

Thank you for taking time to read the enclosed resume. May I highlight the parts most relevant to the position I seek as cruise schedule coordinator?

Your name was given to me at the San Jose Regional Job Fair last week as someone I should contact regarding the Delivery Manager's opening.

For samples of strong lead sentences that are traditional without being boring, look at the letter by Peggy Wilson on the next page and the letter by Larry Alright in the Appendix.

Peggy Wilson, RN

001 N. Arlington • San Ramon, CA 94806 • **(123) 123-1234**

January 15, 199X

Director of Human Resources, Box #92
Chiron Corporation
001 Weaver Street
Emeryville, CA 94608-2916

Without any fanfare, Peggy's concise opening statement leads directly to her qualifications.

Dear Director:

As I've detailed below, the research coordinator position you advertised appears tailor-made for my abilities and background:

YOUR REQUIREMENTS	MY SKILLS
B.S. or M.S. in Biological Science.	B.S.N., 1986; M.S. in progress.
Registered Nurse a plus.	Practicing RN since 1980.
Two years research experience in a pharmaceutical industry.	Currently in second year as a research nurse in drug trial at Kaiser Hospital.
Team player.	Presently collaborate with principle investigators, program coordinators and support staff.
Travel approximately 25% of time.	Experienced international traveler.

I have long been aware of the innovative research being conducted at Chiron, and am enthusiastic about the prospect of using my talents to further your important work.

Thank you for considering my application. I'll call your office next week to see when an interview can be arranged.

Sincerely yours,

Peggy Wilson

Enclosure: resume

The column presentation in this letter makes it easy to see that Peggy more than makes the grade.

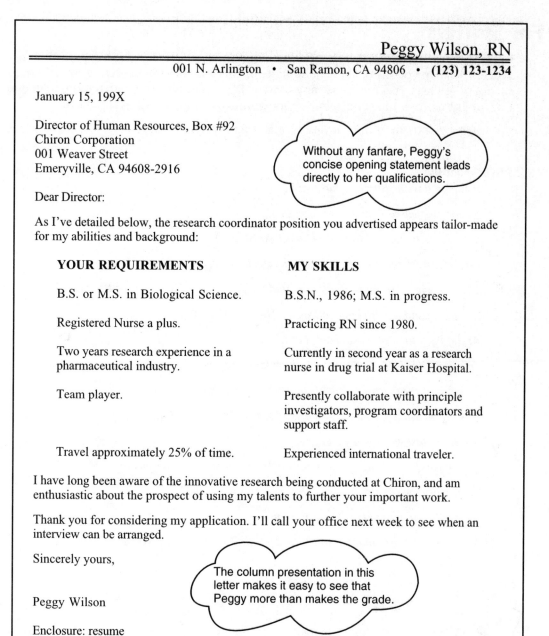

83

For Starters

Coming up with the lead sentence for your letter is one of the toughest steps in this process. To help you think of an appropriate opener for your sales letter, browse through the following lists. Feel free to use any of these lines as is, mix and match more than one line, or just use them to get inspiration for your own award-winning approach.

I've categorized them in three levels: formal, friendly, and bold.

Formal Lingo

You may have a situation that requires...

As an experienced (whatever professional),

In response to your ad in the (whatever newspaper),

I recently read about (some subject relevant to the company).

Your associate, (so-and-so), recently told me (something interesting to the employer).

In a conversation with your colleague, (so-and-so), he told me...

At the suggestion of (so-and-so), I am...

For some time now, I have been looking for an opportunity to (do such-and-such).

Last fall at the (such-and-such) conference, I saw you...

It is my pleasure to re-introduce myself to you. We last met at...

We spoke last when you were...

Thank you for inviting me to submit my resume for (whatever position).

Shortly after we met at the (whatever event), I realized...

(So-and-so) recommended I contact you...

Your assistant, (so-and-so), recently advised me to speak with you about...

Q & A

Is it OK for me to steal ideas or phrases from the list of starting lines in this chapter to use in my letter?

Yes, it is. In fact, that's exactly why I included my list of ideas in this book. If, for some reason, you want to feel "original" while abducting one of my lines, just put a slight twist on it (use your thesaurus to change a word).

Friendly Chat

My career seems to be headed in the direction of (your company).

As the great (whoever) once said, "(quote)."

People say (something-or-other related to your industry).

Everywhere I look, (such-and-such that relates to my work) is happening.

What would happen if (something-or-other that impacts you) took place?

For the last (x) years, (whatever) has been leading to (something-or-other).

Not a day goes by that (something-or-other) doesn't happen.

Last year alone, (x) people did (such-and-such related to the company).

Some people think (something-or-other involving your market).

My clients and friends say...

Developing (such-and-such) is no easy task.

Do you get tired of (something-or-other)?

What does (some concept) have to do with (another, seemingly unrelated concept)?

Remember the good ol' days when...?

Drastic changes are taking place...

In some organizations, things move so quickly that (someone like me) is needed to...Knowing how to (do whatever it is that I do well)...

If you're hesitant to take the step (of doing such-and-such),

"I just can't figure out where to turn for a decent (whatever) professional." Is that what you're saying to yourself?

Just the fact that (some sort of problem has arisen)...

Now that you have my resume in hand,

Once you've read my enclosed resume,

The secret to success in solving (whatever problem) is (my expertise).

You'll be surprised at how promptly (my skills) can turn things around.

When you read my resume, you'll understand how I fit into your program.

Immediate success is what you can expect from my performance as a (whatever).

The very process of finding a (whatever professional), is a job in itself.

For most people,

Once you've had a successful (whatever professional) on your staff, you'll wonder why you delayed...

Believe it or not, (something impressive I've done).

It may seem hard to believe but (some amazing feat you can perform).

When your customers need (whatever), what's the first thing that comes into their minds?

Ever since I can remember,

When you think about it,

Picture (someone doing something or other)...

There's no question,

Ah, the old oxymoron...

When it comes to things we all value...

In today's market...

For those who have my technical background but lack (such-and-such),

One of the biggest problems in today's (whatever market),

If you're looking for special effects in your (whatever) program,

In real estate, the old adage is "location, location, location." Well, in (whatever industry) it's...

As you already know,

Contrary to what most people think,

If you think your customers might not understand (such-and-such), here's how I can help.

No doubt about it,

For openers,

Experienced players in the (whatever) field know that...

Throughout my career as a (whatever), I've...

At first glance, it may appear as though (something isn't right).

The good news is...

To deliver excellent service, I can (do such-and-such).

If you're struggling with (some special problem).

Appealing to your customers' needs is the name of the game.

Looking for a change in the way your company does (whatever)?

When you walk into a store as a customer, how do you measure quality service?

Take it from a pro,

At first glance, (such-and-such about my qualifications) may surprise you, but look closer...

How many times have you (done such-and-such related to your business)?

Tip
Any time you come across clever phrases (in your reading, on TV, during conversation, etc.) that would be good for a cover letter, jot them down. Before you know it, you'll have your own collection of jewels like the ones in this chapter.

Bold Come-on

Call me ambitious, or downright tenacious.

Here's the catch!

What's all the hype?

You may have lights and cameras, but there ain't no movie until there's action.

I can almost feel your grip on this letter tighten as you realize that....

The pitch:

OK, I admit my enthusiasm becomes contagious to almost epidemic proportions.

If you don't remember anything else after reading this letter, remember this:

It's been a long day in the office, you'd like to put on your coat and leave, but wait!

People say I have the most exciting profession in the world—I couldn't agree more.

Write to the Point

You've nabbed the reader with an intriguing lead sentence. Now you need to tell him what job you want.

In the first or at least by the end of the second paragraph, state your job objective. It may be an exact job title, or a proposal to fill a certain role in

Watch Out! CAUTION
Don't tease the employer by making him read too far into your letter to find out what you want—you might lose him altogether. It's easier for a reader to throw away a letter than to work at figuring out its purpose.

the employer's business. Once the employer understands what you're asking for, the contents of your letter will have more meaning to him or her since everything you say in your letter is relevant to your job objective.

The Least You Need to Know

➤ The purpose of the first paragraph is to establish a personal connection with the addressee.

➤ The way you express yourself in the first paragraph sets the tone for the entire letter.

➤ Start the letter with a strong lead sentence, which might mention a familiar name, make a bold claim, offer a business proposition, or ask a question that stimulates immediate interest.

➤ If you have trouble getting your first paragraph started, refer to the list of lead phrases in this chapter.

Chapter 7

Step Three—
The Pitch

In This Chapter

➤ Strategies for constructing a high-scoring middle paragraph

➤ Tips for explaining why you'll be a valuable player on the employer's team

➤ How your letter will stimulate good interview questions

➤ Present your points in an appealing format that will catch the reader's eye and stick in his or her mind

Knowing what you want and why you should have it is half the battle in convincing someone else to give it to you. I don't think any political campaign would have been won if the candidate hadn't bombarded his constituents with reasons he deserved to hold office. Likewise, your letter needs to articulate why you should have the job you're after.

In this chapter, you're going to figure out why you want to work for the employer you have in mind, and why he or she should hire you. Then you're going to present your case in the body of your letter.

What Are You Pitching?

What is your letter selling? You! You're the product, and the middle paragraphs contain your sales pitch. Your confident presentation—a declaration of your job objective (if you haven't already communicated it in your first paragraph) and your qualifications—must convince the reader that you're a good fit for the job.

The following two exercises will help you make a persuasive case.

Tip

The goal of your letter is to turn a monologue (your letter) into a dialogue (an interview) with your prospective employer. To achieve this objective, show sincere interest in your reader's needs, which in turn will spark his interest in you.

Employer's Wish List

"Talk in terms of the other person's interest." That nugget of wisdom comes from the famous teacher of effective sales communications, Dale Carnegie, when he explained the most influential stance for a winning sales pitch.

The middle section of your letter should follow Carnegie's philosophy—tell the reader why you would be a valuable person on his team from his point of view. To prepare yourself for writing this section of your letter, imagine that you are the employer (use the company and hiring manager profiles you created in Chapter 3, "Research Smarts") and answer the following questions.

Q & A

What's an easy way to find out what's required for a job?

Studying a job announcement for the position you're after is an excellent way to know what an employer is looking for in the ideal candidate. Newspapers, telephone job hotlines, on-line job postings, and employment agencies are good sources of such announcements.

BRAINSTORM #1

What skills and experience is the employer looking for in the ideal candidate for the job you wish to fill?

Example:

Someone with 15 years experience in a construction-related field.

Proficiency in traditional and nontraditional architecture.

Budget management and supervisory skills.

Your answer:

1. _____
2. _____
3. _____
4. _____

What personality traits is the employer looking for in the perfect applicant for the position you seek?

Example:

Confident, professional, poised, friendly, firm when necessary.

Ability to pull disparate groups together toward one goal.

Your answer:

1. _____
2. _____
3. _____

OK, now set your lists aside, and let's look at the other side of the coin: what you have to offer the employer.

Measuring Up

As your second step in devising a winning sales pitch for your letter, the next exercise will clarify why you're a good candidate for the job, and reinforce your self-esteem at the same time. Once you've answered the following two questions, you'll be in good shape to present your case to the employer.

Rule

Rule #2: Show Personality. Trying to figure out what personality traits the employer is looking for in an applicant may not be easy. Some ads or job postings say, others don't. If yours doesn't, you'll have to speculate what personality you would hope for in the perfect job seeker if you were the hiring manager.

RULES OF THE ROAD

BRAINSTORM #2

Which of your achievements demonstrate that you have the skills and experience to excel at the job you seek? (Reread Brainstorm #1, exercise #1 to see what qualifications the employer is looking for.)

Example:

> I've worked for the largest architectural firm in the U.S. for 15 years.
>
> I've been the lead architect on more than 14 commercial and residential projects in Japan and the U.S.
>
> I managed design crews and budgets for projects ranging from $6,000 to $4,000,000.

Your answer:

1. _____
2. _____
3. _____

What aspects of your personality would make you a productive member of the team, department, or company? (Refer to Brainstorm #1, exercise #2 to know what characteristics the employer is hoping to find in his new employee.)

Example:

> I'm always chosen as the group representative, due to my ability to present concepts clearly and confidently.
>
> I have a knack for bringing together diverse groups to achieve cooperation in the long- and short-haul.

Your answer:

1. _____
2. _____
3. _____

Q & A

As a CEO, I feel foolish saying that I'm a "responsible" person, even though that's clearly one of my finest personality traits. How can I say it in a way that doesn't sound so obvious?

Instead of saying something like, "I'm a responsible person," you could cite an accomplishment that demonstrates your level of responsibility or you could refer to your work history where your leadership speaks for itself.

One Plus One

Now that you have a list of points the employer is looking for in the ideal candidate and you understand what you have to offer the company, it's time to put these two perspectives together to come up with reasons the employer should want you to work for him or her. To help you articulate those reasons, answer the following questions.

> **Tip**
> A winning cover letter is one that clearly matches an employer's needs with your qualifications.

BRAINSTORM #3

Which points from Brainstorm #1 (what the employer is looking for) match up with the points from Brainstorm #2 (what you have and want to offer the employer)?

Example:

Employer wants #1: Someone with 15 years experience in a construction-related field.

My response #1: I've worked for the largest architectural firm in the U.S. for 15 years.

Employer wants #2: Proficiency in traditional and nontraditional architecture.

My response #2: I've been the lead architect on more than 14 commercial and residential projects in Japan and the U.S..

Employer wants #3: Supervisory and budget management skills.

My response #3: Managed design crews and budgets for projects ranging from $6,000 to $4,000,000.

Employer wants #4: The ideal person for this job is confident, professional, and friendly.

My response #4: I'm always chosen as the group representative, due to my ability to present concepts clearly and confidently.

Employer wants #5: Someone with the ability to pull disparate groups together toward one goal.

My response #5: I have a knack for bringing together diverse groups to achieve cooperation in the long- and short-haul.

NOW, YOUR TURN:

Employer wants #1: _____

Your response #1: _____

Employer wants #2: _____

Your response #2: _____

Employer wants #3: _____

Your response #3: _____

Employer wants #4: _____

Your response #4: _____

Employer wants #5: _____

Your response #5: _____

Hey, your case looks pretty convincing, doesn't it? Now you just have to package it in a paragraph that has graphic appeal.

The Eye Catcher

Make the body of your letter have pizzazz graphically so the reader will want to read it. In other words, make it look quick and easy to read. There are three formats for conveying your qualifications effectively:

➤ Insert bullet points to divide statements into bite-sized pieces.

➤ Design a table that presents your qualifications in column format.

➤ Use short paragraphs.

Let's look at each of these techniques.

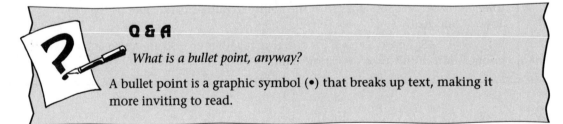

Q & A

What is a bullet point, anyway?

A bullet point is a graphic symbol (•) that breaks up text, making it more inviting to read.

Bullet Points That Hit the Mark

The body of your letter could be comprised primarily of bullet point statements. Bullet points magically draw attention to the sentences that follow them, in your case to your qualifications and achievements. (See Chapter 12, "Announcing, Announcing: Broadcast Letters," to learn how to write strong achievement statements.)

Of course, your bullet points need to be introduced by a short phrase. For example, here is an opening line followed by three bullet point statements:

> *There are a few reasons I would be ideal as the manager of you veterinary clinic:*
>
> - *I was twice recognized by the Veterinary Institute as one of the top five veterinarians in Day County.*
> - *I doubled the profit margins of my practice even when a known franchise veterinary clinic moved into my market.*
> - *I have a strong community presence, having served as councilman for two years.*

There are countless ways to lead into your bullet points of qualifications. Here are some introductory lines I like:

> *Please take a moment to glance at my qualifications for…*
>
> *In addition to what you see on my resume, I have…*
>
> *For a closer look at why I qualify for…*
>
> *In the past eight years I have continually produced impressive results:*
>
> *Here's why I believe I can do the job:*
>
> *Please consider the following:*
>
> *For instance:*
>
> *For example:*
>
> *Relevant achievements:*

Watch Out!
Competition among job seekers for an employer's reading time is fierce. To beat your rivals, use good graphic design to make your most pertinent information "pop out" during a quick initial scan by the employer.

Tip
The structure of bullet point statements in a cover letter may differ slightly from ones on your resume. In your cover letter, you can write complete sentences that use personal pronouns (like "I," "my," and "our"). As a rule, resume statements are not full sentences and do not use personal pronouns. More help on sentence structure appears in Chapter 15, "Good Technique Helps."

Here are some of my achievements:

You'll be interested to know that...

My most notable qualifications are:

Among other accomplishments, I'm proud of:

The following letter (as well as several in the Appendix) show how to give punch to your cover letter by integrating bullet points.

Steve Dobbs

01 Eleanor Place
Redwood City, CA 94040
(123) 123-1234

February 8, 199X

Human Resources Director
Ben and Jerry's Ice Cream
Northern California Headquarters
001 Thorn Street
San Mateo, CA 94036

Bullet points make Steve's achievements jump out on the page!

Dear Director,

As a Personnel Manager, I strive to create an atmosphere of caring, integrity, and professionalism. Ben and Jerry's products and reputation seem to fit my own style to a "T."

My colleagues and managers know me for my:

• Ability to juggle activities and projects -- accomplishing multiple tasks (seemingly) in the blink of an eye.

• In-depth knowledge of medical and health insurance procedures.

• Keen sensitivity to cultural differences -- and the ability to bridge those differences creatively and constructively.

I welcome the opportunity to join your team, and will contact you next week to inquire about a personal meeting. Thank you!

Cherry Garcia forever!

Steve's language has a lot of flavor, even the complimentary close.

Steve Dobbs

Enclosure: resume

So, You Want to Be a Columnist?

Here's an exciting idea: Use a table instead of bullet point statements. Follow the instructions above for leading into bulleted sentences, but instead of using bullet statements, insert two columns: one column for what the employer is looking for; the second column for your qualifications. (That's easy—you already figured out these two perspectives earlier in this chapter when you filled in Brainstorm #3.) Arrange the order of items in the columns so that your qualifications respond to the employer's needs.

For example:

Your Requirements

1. 15 years experience in a construction-related field

2. Proficiency in traditional and nontraditional architecture

3. Supervisory and budget management skills

4. Confident, professional, friendly

5. Ability to pull disparate groups together toward one goal

My Skills

1. 15 years with the largest U.S. architectural firm

2. Lead architect on more than 14 commercial and residential projects in Japan and the U.S.

3. Managed design crews and budgets for projects ranging from $6,000 to $4,000,000

4. Always chosen as the group representative, due to my ability to present concepts clearly and confidently

5. Knack for bringing together diverse groups to achieve cooperation in the long- and short-haul

In the example above, the two column headings are *Your Requirements* and *My Skills*. There are, however, an endless variety of headings that you could use. To come up with column headings you like, choose from one of the following pairs, mix and match to create a set that suits you, or think of a duet on your own:

You Want	I've Got
You Seek	I Offer
Your Ad	My Resume
You Wish	I Bring
You Expect	I Deliver
You Desire	I Possess

Rule

Rule #4: Make It Quick and Easy to Read. To grab the manager's attention (and even make your letter look fun to review), you could insert little "check-off" boxes (❑) in front of each of your qualifications.

Your Needs	I Present
Your Criteria	My Qualifications
Your Job Announcement	My Profile
Your Concerns	My Talents
Your Necessities	My Abilities
Your Goals	My Expertise
Your Objectives	My Competency
Your Challenges	My Record
Your Targets	My Achievements
Your Vision	My Accomplishments
Your Assignment	My Specialties
Your Situation	My Success
Your Game	My Score
Your Mission	My Strengths
You're Stuck	I Can Help
Your New Challenge	I've Done It
The Task	My Merit
The Issue	I Propose
The Problem	I Recommend
Market Trend	I'm Savvy

Nancy's letter, which follows, uses the column concept effectively.

Q & A

I'm having trouble knowing what to say in my letter?

Here's a trick to jostle your mind: Think of what topics you'd like to talk about in your job interview. Then write sentences that tickle interest in those subjects.

NANCY TWEED
001 Los Milagros Road • Lafayette, California 94549 • (123) 123-1234

March 24, 199X

Ms. Kathy Ball
Romano & Teseracci
001 Broadway Avenue
Oakland, CA 94618-2201

Nancy uses two columns to send an immediate message that she has what it takes—and more!

Dear Ms. Ball,

Mick Jagger created a hit with the words, "You can't always get what you want." With all due respect to the Rolling Stones, I beg to differ! In reference to your Training Assistant position, please allow me to demonstrate why:

YOU WANT	I'VE GOT
1. Knowledge of retail or experience in the music industry.	1. Former retail sales associate for Brown's Music Store.
2. Minimum 2 years in training/adult education.	2. Background in teaching, group dynamics, and curriculum development.
3. Excellent oral and written communication skills.	3. Authored training manuals. Used strong interpersonal skills to sell programs.
4. Extroverted and energetic personality.	4. Perform several "dancing bear acts" simultaneously.

Thank you for your time and attention. Shall we talk next week about how we could "make music" together? I'll call your office on Friday to set an appointment.

Nancy uses humor and the turn of a phrase in her letter to emphasize her good-natured personality.

Sincerely yours,

Nancy Tweed

Enclosure: resume

Make It Snappy

You don't have to use bullet points or columns to have a dynamite cover letter. Your letter could be comprised of only paragraphs, with no "fancy" presentations like bullet points or tables. Just make sure your paragraphs are short and loaded with ammunition that sells your product—you!

The brevity of your paragraphs will signal the reader, without her having to read a single word on your page, that your letter is quick to read. Therefore, she'll be inclined to read it *now* rather than setting it aside for when she has free time (which she may never have) or, even worse, just throwing it away.

The following cover letter and several in the Appendix are comprised only of paragraphs (no bullet points or tables). Notice how short the paragraphs are—giving the sense that the letters are quick to get through.

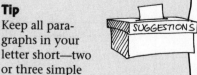

Tip
Keep all paragraphs in your letter short—two or three simple sentences is ideal. (You can find help in simple sentence construction in Chapter 16, "Style Is Everything.")

Watch Out!
A long letter with dense paragraphs is a red flag. It effectively says, "This job seeker is long-winded and doesn't know how to present information in a way that respects the reader's time." Not a good message to send a prospective employer.

Barry Jansen

001 North State Street ✧ Madison, WI 33021 ✧ 123/123-1234

May 12, 199X

Jennifer Taub Abel, General Manager
Autumn Press
001 Twelfth Street, #2
Madison, WI 33026

Short paragraphs give the impression that Barry's letter is a breeze to read.

Dear Ms. Abel,

As a Production Artist with many years' experience in the field, I have a good idea of what you're looking for in an employee. I take tremendous pride in my profession, and can assure you that I share your exacting standards.

I have particular expertise in producing high-quality work under tight deadlines: transforming initial ideas into finished products and using my knowledge of printing to avoid job stalls.

My technical background includes daily experience with graphic arts applications (on both Mac and PC), digital pre-press, and transferring data via the Internet.

All my technical talents wouldn't be of much use to you if I didn't *also* have the teamwork skills which help keep a shop running smoothly, despite conflicting demands. As my bosses have routinely noted, I make it a priority to collaborate with my co-workers, since I see this as the most pleasant, efficient way to work.

There's so much more I could tell you about how I can contribute to Autumn Press -- but I'd much rather do it in person, so I can show you my portfolio, too. I'm available to meet next week -- are you? I'll call you on Tuesday to find out.

I greatly appreciate your consideration.

Sincerely,

Barry Jansen

Enclosure: resume

Barry "marries" his technical and interpersonal skills to fulfill the job qualifications.

The Least You Need to Know

➤ The middle section of your letter should express why you're a strong competitor for the particular job you seek.

➤ Figure out what your selling points are by examining why you want to work for the company and why the employer will want you to work for him or her.

➤ Present your qualifications in one of three formats: short paragraphs, bullet point statements, or columns.

Step Four—
Closing the Sale

So far, your letter has told the employer what type of work you're looking for and why you deserve a shot at a job in her company. Now what? It's time to push for the next move—a job interview.

In this chapter you'll find some techniques for saying "thank you" and asking for a job interview in your last paragraph. Your final words will leave your reader thinking, "I need to talk to this job seeker."

Gotta Say "Thank You"

Everyone loves appreciation, and your prospective employer is no exception. A sincere "thank you" for her having read your letter is appropriate at this point.

Rule

Rule #2: Show Personality. Gratitude—what a great attribute to demonstrate in your cover letter by saying "thank you" to the hiring manager for her time in reading your material.

Don't be gushy with your thanks, and don't grovel. Use a professional note of gratitude that maintains dignity. In other words, instead of "Thank you so much for taking time out of your busy day to see if my qualifications match your job requirements" say something like, "Thank you for considering what I believe is a high-gain situation for us both."

Take a look at the thank yous in the following cover letter and others in the Appendix.

Robert Duncan
01 Onyx Lane, Vallejo, CA 94709
123-123-1234

June 1, 199X

Mr. Jonathan Sachs
Director, Marine Mammal Care
Marine World/Africa U.S.A.
001 Marine World Parkway
Vallejo, CA 94702

> With Robert's friendly, eager approach, his reader can't help but like him.

Dear Mr. Sachs,

I'm enclosing a photo with this letter to show you that my interest in animals goes back -- *way* back. See the toddler trying to climb over the fence to get into the tiger enclosure? Yep, that's me -- although I now know a lot more about what I'm doing with animals (and can do it a lot more safely!)

In high school, I volunteered at the Oakland Zoo three evenings a week, cleaning cages and generally helping out with whatever needed doing. In college, I worked summers at the Marine Mammal Rescue Center. Again, I wasn't fussy; I gladly did my share of the "grunt work," just for the privilege of being near the animals.

Now, with my newly-minted degree in Marine Biology in hand, I'm ready to start wherever you need me -- on land, underwater, or even behind a desk (if that's where you feel you can best use my skills). I know you're doing the most progressive marine mammal research around, and I want to be a part of it!

I really appreciate the time you're taking just to read my letter, as I know you must get many requests like mine. So instead of asking for an interview, I've got a different idea. How about if we meet this Friday, closing time, near the polar bears? Then you can put me to work for the rest of the evening -- sort of a trial run.

Thanks in advance for accepting this offer!

Yours truly,

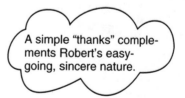

> A simple "thanks" complements Robert's easy-going, sincere nature.

Robert Duncan

Enclosure: resume

The Closer

Closing the deal is where many cover letters fall short. They either fail to ask for the interview, or they meekly suggest the possibility that maybe, just *maybe*, the reader might condescend to talk to the job seeker… *if* it's not too much of an inconvenience. I'm exaggerating, of course. But even an approach as timid as "If after reviewing the enclosed resume you think there might be a job opening that suits my qualifications, you might wish to speak with me" makes you look like a wet noodle.

This is a business letter. You are asking for a business meeting (a job interview) in which you will offer the employer an incredible opportunity to engage in a business transaction (of hiring you) that promises to yield profit for you both. You are not a beggar! You are a confident professional with much to offer. Your confident approach will help convince the employer of your value (which can translate into dollar signs when you negotiate salary).

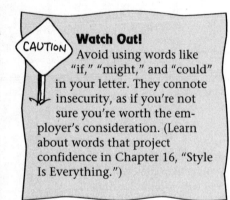

Watch Out!
Avoid using words like "if," "might," and "could" in your letter. They connote insecurity, as if you're not sure you're worth the employer's consideration. (Learn about words that project confidence in Chapter 16, "Style Is Everything.")

Don't Call Me, I'll Call You

Most sales professionals say that if you want a deal to stay alive, *keep the ball in your court*. If that theory works for selling products, it will work for promoting you! In your cover letter, tell your prospective employer that *you* will take the next step (such as telephone or drop by to speak with the reader). An assertive statement such as "I will call your office next week to see when an interview can be arranged" is far more effective than a passive line such as "I look forward to hearing from you." With the passive approach, you could sit by the phone for months never knowing if you're in the running for the job or whether your letter even got to its destination.

The assertive "I'll call you" approach is best because it gives you the opportunity to:

Rule
Rule #3: Initiate Action. You've heard the saying, "If you want a job done right, do it yourself." I've adapted that line a little: "If you want an action taken, take it yourself." Motivate the employer to set up an interview by telling her what *you* plan to do next.

➤ Find out if your letter and resume were received by the employer.

➤ Learn about your status as a job candidate.

➤ Make another personal contact with the employer or someone on his staff.

➤ Decrease the likelihood of your letter and resume getting lost. Alerting the hiring manager (or his administrative assistant) that you will be following up on your application might keep your material within an arm's reach of the reader's telephone—not a bad place for your letter and resume.

Uh Oh, No Phone Number

If all your detective work doesn't turn up a phone number for your addressee, you really can't say "I'll call you" in your closing paragraph. In that case, you need another way to end your letter with intent. Put on your thinking cap and come up with an incentive for the employer to call you right away.

Q & A

Why is it that some company's don't list their phone numbers in their job listings or advertisements?

Companies who don't provide their telephone numbers can save time (and therefore money) by avoiding telephone calls from job seekers. Since job postings and newspaper ads generate such a large response, employers easily find enough qualified applicants *without* having the added cost generated by telephone inquiries.

Here are some possible incentives for an immediate response on the reader's part (of course, use only a reason that is true for you) and some examples of how those reasons might be presented.

1. Boost the Employer's Bottom Line

➤ The reader should seize this opportunity to employ you while he has the chance. You're also applying to his competition.

> *Mr. Richards, I will be honest. Although I have submitted several applications within the plastics manufacturing industry, I am most interested in working as a Quality Assurance Analyst for Dillon Plastics. Please contact me as soon as possible so that we can nail down employment details.*

➤ There is urgency in solving a company problem, and you're the one with the solution.

> *Ms. Pierce, time is slipping by! Please invite me for a meeting to discuss exactly how quickly I can get your production department turned around.*

➤ The industry technology is advancing quickly and you have what it takes to beat the competition—but it must be achieved immediately!

> *Time is critical! If we don't act now, this new motherboard technology will come out on the market under the wrong company name. I'm ready to discuss precise ways of beating your competition to the market. Please call me.*

➤ Every day that the employer delays in hiring you to work on a particular project is costing the employer money.

> *According to my calculations, it costs you roughly $40,000 in revenue every day that we delay in developing this product. Let's get together soon to make plans to get started. Please contact me at _____.*

➤ The employer is anxious to get a specific project (for which you are supremely qualified to direct) underway since the potential for profit is just waiting to be developed.

> *You understand perhaps better than anyone what a gold mine awaits Kevin Bros. in the San Diego market. Every day wasted represents thousands of dollars lost. Please call me about your soonest availability for a meeting.*

➤ The window of opportunity for a product will only be open so long. You can get that product out in time only if you begin right away.

> *With the in-store shelf life of computer manuals as short as it is, we must get your book sales and distribution department working as efficiently as possible. If we can iron out employment details this week, I can come on board next Monday. Please let me know when we can talk.*

➤ The employer has a problem that is growing day by day. You could stop it *now*!

> *As your security manager, I will cut theft to a fraction of what it is now. Please get me on the job before this problem hurts your store image. I can be reached at _____.*

2. Timing Is Everything

➤ You'll be leaving the employer's geographic area on vacation soon. (This assumes that you are applying to a company that is in your locale.)

> *In one week I will leave town for a short trip with my family. An interview prior to my vacation could bring me on board immediately upon my return. Please call me at _____.*

➤ You'll be visiting the employer's geographic area for a limited length of time. (This assumes you are applying to a company that is not near your home.)

> *On July 12th I will be in the Los Angeles area on vacation. It would be an excellent opportunity for us to meet about my proposal. I may be reached in San Francisco at _____ or in Los Angeles at _____ .*

Tip
Don't be afraid to use demonstrative language in your letter—after all, you really want a job from this employer, don't you? Underline, italicize, and make bold the words you want to stress in your text.

Q & A

Won't I look desperate if my letter makes me look too available and eager for an interview?

Desperation is not the impression you want to make with your letter. But the perception of convenience, synchronicity, opportunity—whatever you want to call it—is the effect you want. If your interview makes good business sense with regard to the employer's timing, then your proposal for an interview will sound propitious, not desperate.

➤ You will be in the employer's neighborhood on a certain date for business. You could easily drop by to chat or deliver material.

> *When I am downtown on business Monday, August 9th, I will be free for an interview any time after 10:00 a.m. Please call to let me know what time is convenient for you.*

➤ You realize that the hiring manager is only available for interviews one day of the week. You're ready for a meeting the very next day he is.

> *Your job announcement indicates that you interview only on Fridays. May I secure an appointment for your earliest possible time this Friday? I may be reached at _____ .*

➤ Interviewing takes up a lot of a manager's time. He might as well find the best person (you) now so he can use his time for other business items.

> *Please call me for an interview. I feel confident our meeting will dramatically cut down your need to interview other candidates.*

Notice how the following letter by Blaine O'Henry provides motivation for the employer to call the job seeker.

Blaine O'Henry

001 Geneva Street   123/123-1234   Ann Arbor, MI 48109

January 12, 199X

Jacqueline Black, Manager
Jacobs and Wiley Publishing
001 N. Devere
Detroit, MI 48212

> Instead of saying "excellent communication skills," Blaine uses a relevant example in his first bullet point statement.

Dear Ms. Black,

I was intrigued by your advertisement seeking a Project Writer, as I am certain I can provide the "elegant, fluid conversational style" you need.

Among other qualifications, I offer:

- Extensive writing and publication credentials; recipient of an NEA fellowship and Associated Writing Programs award.
- Proven ability to establish rapport with people of all ages, cultural and economic backgrounds; skilled at drawing out the uniqueness in each person's story.

I am currently finishing up a major freelance project and have several meetings scheduled with clients in the near future. However, I will make every effort to clear time in my schedule next week, so that I can hear more about your project.

Please contact me at your earliest convenience so that we can be assured of arranging a meeting time. Thank you!

Sincerely,

> Blaine creates a sense of urgency for the employer to call him for an interview.

Blaine O'Henry

Enclosure: resume

Finishing Touches

Now that the body of your cover letter is completed, you're ready to finish up. Here's how to sign-off.

Complimentary Close

The complimentary close (like "Sincerely yours") appears immediately after the last paragraph and just before your signature (examine the templates in Chapter 5 for the style of letter you are creating). Each of the following complimentary closes are appropriate for a job search letter:

Sincerely yours,

Sincerely,

Very sincerely,

With regards,

Regards,

What's Your Name Again?

It's customary to leave a few lines blank just below the complimentary close and then type your first and last names. Once your letter emerges from your printer or typewriter, sign your name in that blank space between the complimentary close and your printed name. (More details on ink, spacing, etc. of your signature in Chapter 10, "Wrap It Up.")

Q & A

At the end of my letter, should I sign my first and last names, or just my first name?

Usually one signs his first and last names, but if you are a personal friend of the addressee or have used a very casual style for writing your letter, you could sign just your first name. In that case, the printed name below your signature should give your first and last names.

Many professionals have earned honorary titles such as doctor, professor, or pastor. After receiving a professional title, some professionals like to be called Dr. so-and-so, Professor so-and-so, or Pastor so-and-so, while others of the same stature prefer not to use the titles. If you have a professional title, use your signature to indicate whether or not you wish to be called by your title. Notice the message each of the following signatures conveys:

Dr. James Tyler tells the reader to call him Doctor Tyler.

James Tyler indicates that he prefers to be called James or Mr. Tyler.

Jim Tyler invites a friendly relationship based on nicknames.

James Tyler, Ph.D. leaves the reader in the dark about how the applicant wishes to be addressed—not a good strategy since it might discourage the reader from talking to Mr. Tyler in order to avoid possible embarrassment.

One Last Thing

A few spaces below the signature and flush left on the page, indicate that you are including one or more items (such as your resume) with your letter. Because your cover letter and resume may get separated once it arrives at the company, the "Enclosure" at the bottom of your letter will alert the reader that your resume is somewhere in the building.

Rule

Rule #4: Make It Quick and Easy to Read. A notice of enclosure at the very end of your cover letter immediately sends the desired message that this is a letter regarding a job application.

The following examples demonstrate correct styles for presenting your enclosure notice:

Enclosure: resume

Enclosures: resume and sample article

Enclosures: resume

sample article

The Least You Need to Know

➤ Close your letter on an assertive professional note.

➤ Thank the employer for his or her time in reviewing your qualifications.

➤ Ask for an interview.

➤ When possible, keep the ball in your court by telling the reader that you will follow-up with a phone call or personal visit.

➤ If you aren't able to get the employer's phone number, use a strong remark that gives incentive to the employer to contact you.

➤ End your letter with a complimentary close, your name, and "Enclosure" to note that you have included your resume or other materials.

Part 3
Getting the Right Message Into the Right Hands

You've been sailing right along with your letter writing, haven't you? You cast your message with a terrific lead sentence, hooked your reader with an irresistible sales pitch, and reeled him in with a strong closer.

Except for tying a few loose ends, your letter project is done. Seeing that the big catch is almost yours, you may be tempted to ignore the loose ends and let them flap in the breeze. But wait... given one more twist, those ends could tie into some unforeseen benefits.

While you still have your writing momentum, check out the following chapters to learn about some finishing touches that you may not have thought of. Yes, that means you might need to expend one more ounce of energy. But when that ounce of energy comes back to you in the form of a winning job offer or business connection, you'll be able to brag about what a big fish you caught!

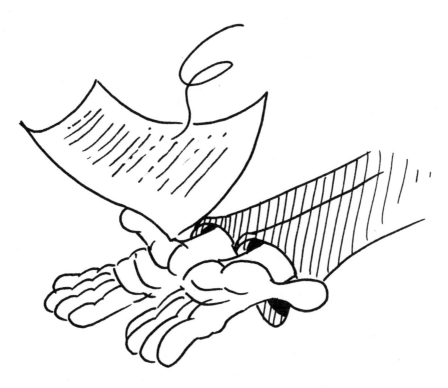

Chapter 9

Sticky Situations

In This Chapter

➤ How to respond to a job ad that requests your salary history

➤ Present your career change as an asset to your future employer

➤ Tips on dealing with your current unemployment status

➤ Strategies for parents reentering the workforce

➤ How to use your letter to avoid age discrimination

➤ How to ask the reader to maintain confidentiality about your job search

➤ What not to put in your cover letter

Some of the most beautiful roses have the largest thorns, right? Flower arrangers learn how to handle those sticky buggers to create gorgeous bouquets.

If you're worried about thorny issues like a career change, request for salary history, age discrimination, or unemployment, take it easy—this chapter has some answers for how to handle them in your cover letter.

When you're done with your letter, your qualifications will be appreciated like a bouquet of roses—all the attention will be on the flowers instead of the thorns.

Let's Talk Money... or Maybe Not

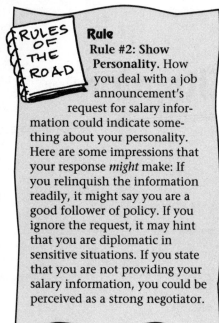

Rule

Rule #2: Show **Personality.** How you deal with a job announcement's request for salary information could indicate something about your personality. Here are some impressions that your response *might* make: If you relinquish the information readily, it might say you are a good follower of policy. If you ignore the request, it may hint that you are diplomatic in sensitive situations. If you state that you are not providing your salary information, you could be perceived as a strong negotiator.

Although some job advertisements ask for a resume and salary information, the two do not go together. Ideally, discussion about salary belongs in the interview, not on the resume. It is greatly to your advantage not to make a monetary request before an interview. Indicating salary requirements before the interview may increase your chances of being screened out, and decrease your bargaining power during salary negotiations.

Take a Risk

You know what I would do if faced with the kind of demand for salary information mentioned above? I'd flat-out ignore the request. That's right, I'd take the risk that even though I didn't respond to the ad's requirement, I'd still get in the door for an interview. I say "risk" because there *would be* a risk in not complying since I could be disqualified for being "insubordinate." But, there would also be a risk if I *did* comply, since I could easily be screened out for asking for too much money. Personally, I would prefer the first gamble to the second mentioned above. Of course, you need to decide which suits your style of risk-taking.

Q & A

Should I or shouldn't I even mention the word "salary" in my letter?

There's no right or wrong answer to that question. Read my advice in this section and do what your intuition tells you is right for your situation—and do it confidently!

Walking on Golden Eggs

If you feel obligated to address salary history in order to fulfill the employer's initial application requirements, do so in your cover letter (not on your resume!). Speak in generalities such as:

My salary in previous positions ranged from $X to more than $Y, accompanied by benefits.

My growth in earnings from $4.25 an hour as a grocery clerk back in 1986 to my current salary as a division manager is something I'm extremely proud of.

Since salary history is a confidential matter, please understand that I prefer to speak about it in person.

I would like to discuss my salary history during our interview.

Frank's letter, on the following page, demonstrates one way to side-step the salary history question.

Tip
Sometimes the notice "please send salary history" (or something close to that) is put in a help wanted ad by the human resources department without the hiring manager's knowledge. In such cases, the manager is not likely to hold it against an applicant for not including salary information along with his resume and cover letter.

119

FRANK ANSEL, M.P.H.
001 Fremont Boulevard
Union City, New York 21467
123/123-1234

March 11, 199X

Mr. Paul Drew
Albany Public Health Department
001 North Sycamore Street
Albany, NY 21402

Frank's salutation indicates that he is on a first name basis with the reader.

Dear Paul,

Thanks for sending me the job description for the Community Health Educator position. My resume is enclosed.

The position sounds ideal for me, as I have extensive experience in the areas required: developing and conducting trainings, creating and disseminating educational messages, and establishing trust and dialogue with diverse communities.

• At the WASHTENAW COUNTY CLINIC, I delivered trainings and program support to numerous community-based organizations.

• Working with AIDSCOM, I quickly established rapport with AIDS Program Staff in other countries, providing highly effective technical assistance.

• For the NORTHERN G.A.P. PROJECT, I coordinated a school-based AIDS education program for youth, interfacing with teachers, parents and community leaders.

My salary in the above positions has varied considerably, due to the fluctuations in funding available to community-based organizations. I am always willing to negotiate with prospective employers to ensure that our mutual needs can be met.

I look forward to speaking with you more about the position, and will call your office next week to schedule a time for us to meet. It'll be nice to see you again!

Yours truly,

Frank cleverly speaks of his salary history without revealing any figures.

Frank Ansel

Enclosure: resume

Know Your Stuff

Talking directly about salary expectations in a letter is tricky. I suggest that you first find out what the position typically pays. (Learn about pay scales by checking with a career counselor; an employment agency; ads for similar job offers in the newspaper; and on-line resources.) Then mention your salary expectations in your cover letter using language that gives you room for negotiations, such as "I am looking for a position in the $X to $Y salary range."

Here's how Lisa dealt with the salary expectation issue in her letter.

Tip

When the sit-down-hammer-it-out salary negotiations start, remember this terrific bargaining technique called *cherry picking*: Present a number of items you want as part of the deal, knowing that you probably won't get everything on your wish-list. The employer, feeling pretty smart about his bargaining skills, will likely pick a few "cherries" from your list and reject the rest. You both come out of the bargaining room smiling, feeling that a real compromise was made.

Tip

Salary negotiating is a skill in and of itself. Your cover letter and resume will get you the interview; your interview should get you to the bargaining table; your negotiations should win you your desired compensation. For help tuning up your negotiating skills, refer to *The Complete Idiot's Guide to the Perfect Job Interview* and practice interviewing with a friend or counselor.

LISA GREEN

001 West Mesa Drive ✪ Tucson, AZ 22341 ✪ 123/123-1234

April 30, 199X

Ms. Sandra Hernandez, Director
Women's Choice Clinic
001 North Prickly Pear Road
Tucson, AZ 22352

> Lisa makes a political statement that supports her job objective.

Dear Ms. Hernandez,

Fighting for women's reproductive freedom is my passion in life. My "weapons" are:

- Compassion, empathy, dedication and *respect.*
- Fluency in Spanish; some knowledge of Navajo. Awareness of (and sensitivity to) nuances of Native American and Latin American cultures.
- Strong listening and assessment skills.
- A fiery tongue, a willingness to cross picket lines, a brave heart, and (can you believe it's necessary to say this in America in 1997?!) a bulletproof vest...

I know you may have struggled with staff attrition lately -- it's a scary time. But I can assure you, I'm in this for the long haul.

I'm also extremely flexible. I'd consider a job as an advocate...group leader... counselor...outreach coordinator...or any other non-medical position you have available.

As for my salary expectation, I propose something similar to the arrangement at my last job: I started at a basic hourly rate; then I identified and helped secure additional funding sources, enabling my employer to double my wages. (The grant I brought in also allowed us to add more evening hours.)

I am eager to talk with you about how we can work together. I'll stop by your office next Tuesday, after the Pro-Choice Rally, to set up an appointment.

In solidarity,

> Lisa addresses her salary expectations without spilling the beans about how much she hopes to make.

Lisa Green

Enclosure: resume

New Beginnings

Changing your career? If so, you're not alone. Did you know that on average, Americans change careers *nine times* during their adult life? That's right. Even though career transition is common, it still becomes an issue for some employers. For that reason, you need to consider how you're going to deal with your career change in your cover letter. Here are two ways of dealing with the situation:

1. Focus on your strengths and ignore the fact that you're changing careers.

2. Address your career change head-on in your letter, framing it as a tremendous asset that other applicants probably don't have.

Either method is acceptable. Let's look at each of these two solutions so that you can decide which suits your style of communication.

Closing Your Eyes to Change

In the "ignore" game plan (point #1, above), don't even mention in your letter the fact that the position you seek is not in your previous line of work. Instead, emphasize all the skills, achievements, and attributes that are common to both your former and future jobs. The goal of this strategy is to spotlight the positive to such an extent that your career change (which could possibly be perceived as a negative) is not immediately noticed by the employer.

Alison Levine's letter on the following page is a typical example of ignoring a career change. From her letter alone, it is impossible to know that she has changed careers three times.

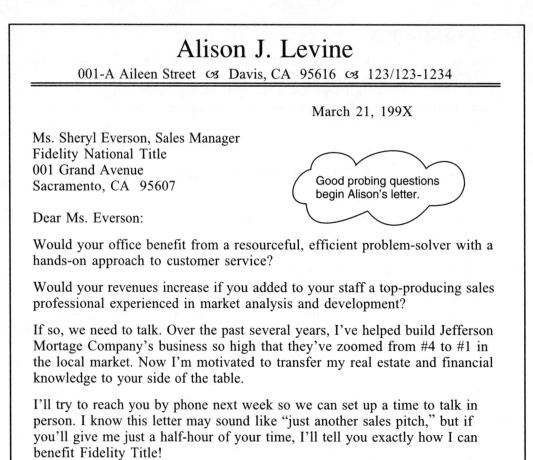

Alison J. Levine

001-A Aileen Street ❧ Davis, CA 95616 ❧ 123/123-1234

March 21, 199X

Ms. Sheryl Everson, Sales Manager
Fidelity National Title
001 Grand Avenue
Sacramento, CA 95607

Good probing questions begin Alison's letter.

Dear Ms. Everson:

Would your office benefit from a resourceful, efficient problem-solver with a hands-on approach to customer service?

Would your revenues increase if you added to your staff a top-producing sales professional experienced in market analysis and development?

If so, we need to talk. Over the past several years, I've helped build Jefferson Mortage Company's business so high that they've zoomed from #4 to #1 in the local market. Now I'm motivated to transfer my real estate and financial knowledge to your side of the table.

I'll try to reach you by phone next week so we can set up a time to talk in person. I know this letter may sound like "just another sales pitch," but if you'll give me just a half-hour of your time, I'll tell you exactly how I can benefit Fidelity Title!

Thank you.

Sincerely,

Alison never mentions that she has changed careers three times.

Alison Levine

Enclosure: resume

Touting Your Career Change News

This is a much bolder approach: Announce your career transition as a unique bonus that other job candidates don't have—the perfect marriage of skills and achievements that could have been accumulated in no better way. In this letter, your confidence shines through and you openly invite the reader to see you as better than your competition.

Take a look at the following letter (as well as the one by Larry Hilton in Chapter 6) to see this approach in action.

Tip
Writing a strong letter that convinces the reader that your career change is an asset to your next job will have added benefit to you—it will boost your confidence and help you articulate your career move in your interview.

Scot Belmont

0001 Reed Avenue • Davis, CA 95616 • 123/123-1234

May 2, 199X

Ms. Jazmin Medina
Translation Services
Stanford University Hospital
01 University Ave.
Palo Alto, CA 95608

> In his fourth paragraph, Scot states that he is making a career change, while demonstrating his transferable skills.

Dear Ms. Medina,

I have a passion for helping people to better understand the health issues that affect their lives -- and the sensitivity and communication skills to convey such an understanding.

The attached resume documents my work history. However, what's harder to demonstrate on paper is my intimate familiarity with what your ad calls "the cultural/perceptual factors that may have an effect on patient treatment and communication."

One of my best friends is Mexican and HIV-positive. My wife, who is Puerto Rican, is a long-term diabetic who recently underwent a kidney transplant. My experiences helping these and other people close to me to navigate the health care system have contributed immeasurably to my skill and commitment as a health care Spanish-language translator.

Although the bulk of my professional experience has been in the administrative field, the work I've done is closely related to your program's needs. I've made numerous trips to Latin America where I served as a conduit between my boss and his Chilean partners – facilitating complex communications, just as I would between patients and their doctors.

I am excited by the idea of using my talents to benefit a world-class facility like Stanford University Hospital. I'll contact you next week to see when we could meet. Thank you.

Sincerely,

> Scot relies heavily on unpaid work experience to support his job objective.

Scot Belmont

Enclosure: resume

Speaking of Unemployment

Most of us have taken time off during our careers—sometimes by choice, sometimes not by choice. In either case, no matter how wonderful it seemed to you when you weren't doing the daily nine-to-five thing, an employer might not view it with approval.

Q & A

If, in my cover letter, I don't say that I'm recently unemployed, will that be considered telling a lie?

No, nondisclosure is not the same as lying. When the time is right, you will tell the employer that you are not currently employed. Until that time, you are not obligated to reveal your employment status.

Employers don't like to see a gap in your work history, particularly if the gap is current and long-term. They would rather see the unemployed time explained, especially if the explanation is somehow connected to your job objective, or at least shows strength of character.

The best place to justify gaps in your employment history is on your resume. (For help with addressing gaps in your work history, refer to my book, *The Complete Idiot's Guide to the Perfect Resume.*) You are not obligated to speak of work gaps in your cover letter, although you may want to if you are currently unemployed, have been so for quite some time, and you were unable to disguise your jobless state on your resume.

If you're presently unemployed, here are some ways to deal with it in your cover letter:

➤ Consider all the things you are doing while currently unemployed (volunteer work, school activities, internships, schooling, travel, etc.) and present it in a way that's relevant to your job objective, if possible.

Someone looking for a medical sales position who took care of an ill parent for two years might say: "I am currently a home care provider for a terminally ill relative."

An applicant for a travel agent position could refer to their vacation: "I have just returned from travel to Europe, Asia, and South America."

Watch Out!
CAUTION
A long, unexplained void in your work history may cause the reader to think, "This person is hiding something" or "Here's someone who might have a problem" (such as substance abuse, incarceration, laziness, or instability). To gain the employer's trust, it's important to justify your employment gaps.

Watch Out!
Don't refer to illness, unemployment (even if it is clearly due to a recession), or rehabilitation. These topics usually raise red flags, so avoid mentioning them at all cost. Refer to something else you are doing, even if it doesn't relate to your job objective.

CAUTION

A mother wanting to reenter the job market as a teacher's aide might say: "For the last three years, I have been a full-time parent and active PTA volunteer at St. John's Academy." (More about reentry parents coming right up in this chapter.)

➤ If your activities during your unemployment have no apparent relevancy to your job objective, I suggest you either avoid talking about it in your letter altogether (a method I mentioned for career changers in the "New Beginnings" section of this chapter) or explain what you are doing in a way that is honest and feels comfortable to you.

Here's a list of activities you might not think of:

Volunteer *whatever*	Freelance *whatever*
Independent study	Consultant
Personal travel	Contractual *whatever*
Adventure travel	Relocation from abroad
Professional development	Volunteerism
Student	Civic leadership

Q & A

Do I have to say "volunteer program coordinator" when I refer to my work at the Junior League?

You have the license to say "volunteer program coordinator" or just "program coordinator." Since your letter is not a confessional, you don't have to disclose whether or not you were paid for your service.

The following letters by Andres Mejilla and by Lynn Powell, (in the Appendix), have something in common: They address current gaps in employment. If you're looking for a way to justify unemployment, one of their letters may give you an idea for handling your situation.

Andres Mejilla

001 Lazaro Way   Phone: 123/123-1234
Orlando, FL 33229   Voicemail: 123/123-1235

August 1, 199X

Ms. Yvonne Lucky
Director, International Division
BAR Manufacturing, Inc.
01 Coral Highway
Miami, FL 30340

> Andres shows that he's done his homework and knows what this reader needs.

Dear Ms. Lucky,

Does BAR Manufacturing have the potential to double -- even triple -- its number of international licensees within one year?

Having examined your company's products, track record and current performance, I believe that you do -- but only with the correct senior executive on board.

My track record in international marketing, market development and licensing speaks for itself (please see my enclosed resume). And, of course, my extensive contacts in U.S. and foreign embassies and commerce departments help facilitate business.

The take-home message? I can help your business soar.

Since I left Mohr, Inc. late last year to take care of some pressing family matters, I am available to start work immediately. I'll call you next week so we can talk more about when, where and how. Thank you.

Sincerely yours,

> Diplomatically, Andres mentions his current unemployment.

Andres Mejilla

Enclosure: resume

Leaving Home... for the Second Time

Many adults who find themselves reentering the workforce after one or many years of child rearing are puzzled about their place in the current job market. If you're a reentry job hunter, you're probably scratching your head and asking questions like:

➤ How do I explain so many years of "not working"?

➤ Do I have the skills to compete in the current world of employment?

➤ How do I market myself to an industry that has been zooming ahead while I was busy changing diapers, shuttling kids, and doing volunteer work?

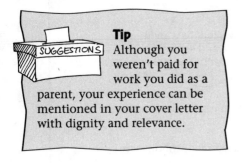

Tip
Although you weren't paid for work you did as a parent, your experience can be mentioned in your cover letter with dignity and relevance.

Before you put any energy into your job search, you need to get one thing straight: Your role as a parent, family manager, community volunteer, student, or freelance worker (to mention just a few of the things you might have been doing while your kids learned how to walk) is valuable and marketable to an employer. In these roles, you maintained and developed skills, many of which are relevant to your new job objective.

A Woman's Work Is Never Done

Raising a family is hard work, requiring many skills. I don't need to tell you that—*you* of all people know! To prepare for your job search, make a list of the skills it took (or takes) to be the good parent you are. Your skill list might include:

Problem solving	Nutrition
Organization	Counseling
Driving	Negotiating
Financial management	Remodeling
Scheduling	Project management
Teaching	Event planning
Caregiving	Communications
CPR	Record keeping
Cooking	Policy development

Ready to make your list? Here you go…

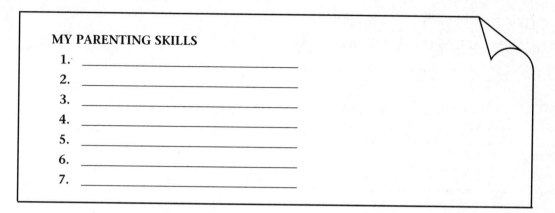

MY PARENTING SKILLS

1. _____
2. _____
3. _____
4. _____
5. _____
6. _____
7. _____

In your skills inventory above, check off the ones that are relevant to your new job.

Great! Now you know what your marketable skills are from your family management experience.

Volunteerism Pays Off

Use your volunteer experience proudly in your cover letter (and resume) to demonstrate that you have the skills, experience, personality, and, yes, passion (perhaps for a relevant social cause or humanitarian effort) for the job you seek. To help you realize what skills you've developed through your community service, take a look at the following talents used by many volunteers:

Rule
Rule #2: Show Personality. Many employers feel that what a job seeker does for no pay speaks louder about her character and commitment than what she does for money.

RULES OF THE ROAD

Staff supervision

Volunteer coordination

Fundraising (aka: "development" in the nonprofit world)

Event planning

Public relations

Scheduling

Counseling

Customer service

Program design

Curriculum development

Caregiving

Communications

Writing

Graphic design

Sales

Training

Now make a list of skills *you* used (or use) in your community service.

MY SKILLS FROM VOLUNTEER WORK

1. _____
2. _____
3. _____
4. _____
5. _____
6. _____
7. _____

Again, check off the skills that will be useful in your new job.

See how much you have to offer an employer? Lots! You just have to talk confidently about them in your cover letter.

The following letter is written by Susan Hamilton, a woman reentering the job market after raising a family of four over the last 17 years.

Susan Hamilton
001 Dorston Way
Boston, MA 92113
☎ 123/123-1234

March 15, 199X

Mr. Paul James
Director of Human Resources
James, Royal & Johnson
0001 Market Street, Ste. 700
Boston, MA 92034

Dear Mr. James,

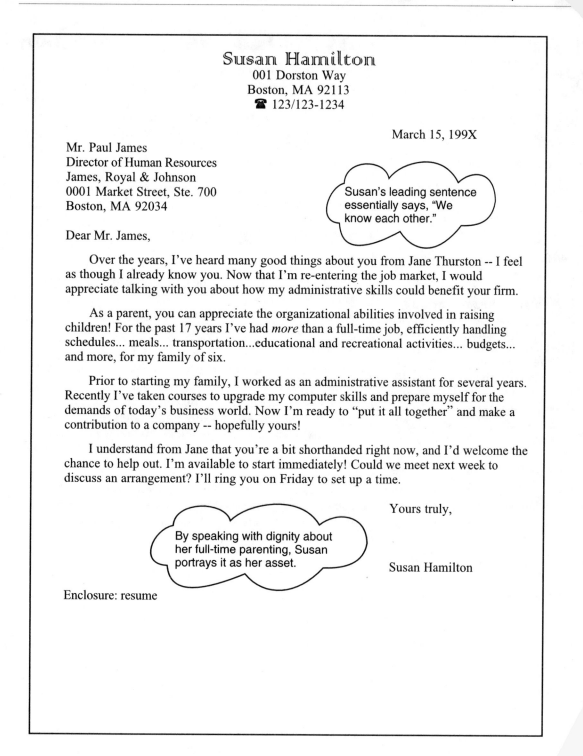

Susan's leading sentence essentially says, "We know each other."

Over the years, I've heard many good things about you from Jane Thurston -- I feel as though I already know you. Now that I'm re-entering the job market, I would appreciate talking with you about how my administrative skills could benefit your firm.

As a parent, you can appreciate the organizational abilities involved in raising children! For the past 17 years I've had *more* than a full-time job, efficiently handling schedules... meals... transportation...educational and recreational activities... budgets... and more, for my family of six.

Prior to starting my family, I worked as an administrative assistant for several years. Recently I've taken courses to upgrade my computer skills and prepare myself for the demands of today's business world. Now I'm ready to "put it all together" and make a contribution to a company -- hopefully yours!

I understand from Jane that you're a bit shorthanded right now, and I'd welcome the chance to help out. I'm available to start immediately! Could we meet next week to discuss an arrangement? I'll ring you on Friday to set up a time.

Yours truly,

By speaking with dignity about her full-time parenting, Susan portrays it as her asset.

Susan Hamilton

Enclosure: resume

It's Not Fair—Age Discrimination

Most employers have an age range they consider to be ideal for a particular job, based on salary expectations, skill level, ability to supervise or be supervised, and amount of life experience needed. A well-written letter uses reference to time spans to lead the employer to deduce that you are at least the ideal age for the job you're after, regardless of your actual age.

The following two sections show you how to work with time spans in your cover letter to create the ideal image.

How to Look Younger

Alice, 56, is applying for a job as a data entry operator in a credit union. She thinks the employer is probably looking for a woman in her late 20s since the employer wants someone who is proficient on the computer, yet won't expect wages as high as someone who has had a long career.

To present herself in her cover letter as the ideal candidate, Alice decides to speak only about the last nine years in her work history, since the employer will most likely take 20 years old as a starting point, add the nine years of work experience she writes about, and conclude that Alice is *at least* 29 years old. Likewise, on her resume, she has been careful not to include dates more than nine years ago, so as not to give away her exact age.

The sentence "I have been in data entry for nine years" in Alice's letter is honest, it just doesn't tell all. In the interview she will have the opportunity to sell herself with her enthusiasm, professional manner, and appropriate salary request—thereby fulfilling the employer's expectations of the ideal candidate.

Here's the letter Alice wrote to accompany her resume.

Watch Out!
CAUTION Age discrimination is illegal, but like it or not, employers usually try to figure out your age using the dates and numbers of years of experience you give in your letter and resume.

Watch Out!
CAUTION Age discrimination works both ways—too old and too young. For one job, you may be perceived as being too young; for another position, you might be considered too old. If you sincerely believe you can and want to do the job, use the age formula in this section to get a fair shake at being hired.

ALICE GREY
001 GRIMSHAW ✱ YPSILANTI, MI 48204 ✱ 123/123-1234

June 2, 199X

Ms. LaRhonda Crosby
Personnel Manager
University of Michigan Credit Union
001 Third Street
Ann Arbor, MI 48109

By saying "nine years in data entry," Alice tells the employer that she's at least 29 years old. She's actually 56.

Dear Ms. Crosby:

Ruth Elsner, who knows my work and qualifications well, suggested I contact you regarding a position in Data Management.

I have been in data entry for nine years, and am thoroughly familiar with the requirements of the field. My past employers have commended me for my highly organized work habits and extremely low error rate.

I'm also a conscientious team player with the ability to inspire my co-workers to greater productivity and cooperation. I enjoy learning, and am always amenable to taking on new challenges.

I have enclosed my resume, and would appreciate the chance to discuss my experience and skills with you in person. I'll call your office next week to see about a time.

Thank you for examining my qualifications.

To ensure a response, Alice says she will call the reader.

Most sincerely yours,

Alice Grey

Enclosure: resume

Creating an Older Image

Don is a new grad who has worked in sales positions all through high school and college. He's a remarkable achiever and is ready for more responsibility on the sales force than most his age. He applies for a position as a regional sales manager, knowing that if he can just get his foot in the door he can convince the boss he can handle the job.

He decides that the employer is probably expecting to hire someone in his late 20s. So in his letter (on the following page), Don refers to his experience eight years ago when he started working for his dad in his retail store, as well as sales achievements at other places of employment. On his resume, he states that he has a degree, but does not give the date since it might indicate that he is only 22.

Everything in Don's letter honestly paints the picture of someone who has the experience and maturity of a 28-year-old without ever saying his age.

Q & A

Is there an easy formula to help me make the kind of impression I want to regarding my age?

Yes. I call it my EPT formula (Experience Plus Twenty). Add the number of years of experience stated to 20 (as a ballpark figure for how old you *might* have been when your experience started) to get a total of x. That means you are at least x years old.

For instance, a letter written in 1997 that talks about experience dating back to 1981, tells the reader that the job applicant is at least 36 years old. (16 years experience plus 20 equals 36—that's the EPT formula.)

DON BLACK

001 Mandana Drive, #311 • Oakland, CA 94610
123/123-1234

March 30, 199X

Ms. Carmen Song, District Manager
Peet's Coffee and Tea
001 Lakeshore Avenue
Oakland, CA 94610

> Although Don is only 22, he refers to experience eight years ago, giving the impression that he's as mature as a 28-year-old.

Dear Ms. Song:

Nothing beats a Peet's cafe latte to get me going in the morning... or a steaming cup of Earl Grey to mellow me out in the afternoon. In addition to the high-quality beverages you serve (definitely the best around), I've always appreciated the lively, progressive atmosphere of your stores, and your commitment to community involvement. That's why I'm determined to become your Regional Sales Manager.

My career in retail sales began eight years ago, when I discovered I had a natural talent for what's known as "consultive sales." I consistently turn relaxed, genuine conversations about customers' needs into sales. Moreover, my credibility, warmth and product knowledge ensures return business.

Specifically, my sales accomplishments include:
• Beat monthly sales goals by as much as 300%.
• Trained and mentored the highest producing sales team in store history.
• Rapidly ascended from Sales Associate to Sales Manager at Cuppa Joe, a coffee/tea specialty store in the Orlando area.

I am eager to demonstrate what an asset I could be on your team. Thank you for reviewing my resume, and I'll call you next week to see about an interview time.

Sincerely yours,

> Don's letter beams with enthusiasm and commitment. Good qualities for an employee.

Don Black

Enclosure: resume

Shhh! My Job Search Is a Secret

If you're currently employed, you may not want your boss to know about your job search. Most potential employers automatically understand and respect a job seeker's need for confidentiality. There are, however, no guarantees that an employer will be discreet on your behalf. If you are particularly concerned about maintaining your job hunt privacy, you could insert a sentence in your cover letter that specifically requests that your present employer not be notified. For example:

> *For reasons of confidentiality, I would appreciate it if you did not contact my current employer until you and I have spoken in person.*

Notice how Tim Crestwood requested discretion in his letter on the following page.

But sometimes asking someone not to spill the beans doesn't work. Without knowing how it happened, you could find your boss steaming mad, all because he found out you're pounding the streets looking for a job. Here are some ways word of your job hunt could leak to the wrong people:

➤ Gossip travels fast in close-knit industries and professions. The news of your job search might get to your current boss through his professional grapevine.

➤ If you're responding to a job announcement that does not give the name of the employer, you could find yourself unknowingly soliciting a job from your current employer. Oops! Cat's out of the bag!

Alex Beckenridge's letter also demonstrates how to conduct a job search discreetly.

Tim Crestwood
01 Royal Oak Drive, #206 ◆ San Jose, CA 95034

Voicemail: 123/123-1234

Email: Timcrest@deltacom.com

June 29, 199X

Mr. Yusef Naik, CEO
Golden Key Products, Inc.
001 Edinburgh Parkway, Ste. 400
San Jose, CA 95011

Tim's winning cards are on the table in his first paragraph.

Dear Mr. Naik:

For 19 years I have been a player in the Silicon Valley phenomenon. As Director of Operations of a high-tech leaders, I've been instrumental in the startup, growth, downsizing, and now complete turn-around of a $3 billion hardware manufacturer.

Yes, there were times when I wasn't sure about the future of our economy, but I never doubted that computer technology was here to stay. And I never stepped out of the inner circle of executive management, because I knew the key to our success lay in the power of the human mind.

Which leads me to what I can offer you. As your Director of Operations, I can pour all my expertise into developing your company into a giant. I've done it before -- and I can do it again... for you!

I would like to sit down for a private conversation with you. Are you free next week? I'll give you a call to set a time. Until then, I ask that you keep this application confidential. Thank you.

Sincerely yours,

Tim Crestwood

Enclosure: resume

Tim directly asks the employer not to disclose his job search.

Alex Beckenridge
001 Luna y Sol Drive
San Diego, CA 92033
123-123-1234

June 1, 199X

Mr. George Robertson
Greenridge Golf Course
001 Dorado Parkway
La Jolla, CA 92341

> Alex explains his need to apply anonymously for the job.

Dear Mr. Robertson:

Turf management is a skill I've honed over the last nine years. I was fortunate to begin my career under the mentorship of a truly fine professional in golf course management.

Our industry is a small one — it's likely that we have mutual business associates. So as not to jeopardize my current position, I am submitting my resume under a pseudonym and with generalized employer "names."

I have many questions about how our interests match, as I'm sure you do. As soon as I receive written acknowledgment of this packet, I trust we can begin an open dialogue about how my expertise can enhance ground operations at Greenridge.

I will await your reply. Thank you!

Sincerely,

> Quotes around his "name" acknowledge that it is not his real name.

"Alex Beckenridge"

Enclosure: resume

What Should be Missing from Your Missive

In the last several chapters, I've told you what to put in your letter. Now let's talk about what to leave out.

Don't Play It Again, Sam

Many think that your cover letter should summarize your resume. Not so! This concept may surprise you, but think about it—you spent at least three hours creating a resume that summarizes your relevant achievements and qualifications. Why would you turn around and do it again in your cover letter, which accompanies your resume?

This "no summary" concept applies only to cover letters, not to broadcast letters, which are explained in Chapter 12.

Tip
Your cover letter is not a confessional. That means you don't have to tell all—you get to leave off information if it's not appropriate or doesn't support your job objective.

In Reference to References

Addresses and phone numbers of references should not be a part of your cover letter. They belong on a separate sheet of paper that you bring to the job interview.

Hey Boss, Mind Your Own Business

Including information about your age, sex, marital status, and health in your cover letter or resume is not appropriate when applying for a job in the United States. If you are applying abroad (in Europe or the United Kingdom), however, it might be expected.

Watch Out!
Don't summarize your resume in your cover letter. Your resume already says why you would be good at a certain job. Your cover letter should take that thought one step farther by pinpointing why you fit into the company you wish to work for.

The Least You Need to Know

➤ Avoid responding to a request for your salary history in your cover letter.

➤ If you decide you *must* talk about salary issues, refer to them in vague terms so you don't reveal too much information.

➤ A safe way to deal with a career change in your letter is to ignore it all together; a bolder approach is to sell your transition as a valuable asset.

➤ Avoid age discrimination by being conscious of how many years of experience you state.

➤ Disguise your current unemployment by referring to unpaid activities that support your job objective, when possible.

➤ Your cover letter should not summarize your resume; your letter should serve as a companion to your resume.

➤ Items that should not appear in your cover letter include references and personal data.

Wrap It Up

In This Chapter

➤ A check list to ensure your finished letter is absolutely perfect

➤ Make a stunning impression with professional layout

➤ How to sign your masterpiece

➤ Tips on handling the outer wrapping—your envelope

➤ When to use mail, courier, fax, and e-mail to deliver your letter and resume

➤ How to request a promotion within your current company

Congratulations! You've done a fine job of composing a sales letter about yourself. You look so good, your competition doesn't stand a chance!

This chapter is going to give you the added confidence that you've crossed all your T's and dotted all your I's. It also gives you ideas about how to produce and mail your letter so it gets into the right hands.

Checklist

Get out your magnifying glass and take a long look at your letter to make sure you haven't forgotten anything. Sharpen your pencil and check off each of the following items:

❑ Your name appears in the letterhead in the top center or on the upper-right side (not in the upper-left corner) of the page.

❑ Your letter is addressed to the hiring manager, the director of human resources, or to someone in the company who you personally know.

❑ Your letter starts with a strong lead sentence that engages the reader immediately.

❑ You quickly establish a personal connection with the reader by referencing a friend, associate, or area of interest common to you both.

❑ The text of your letter gives the reader a sense of your personality.

❑ Your letter sells the reader on the prospect of you working for him or her.

❑ The closing paragraph initiates a next step such as an interview.

❑ Your cover letter refers to an enclosed resume.

❑ Your letter fits on one page and looks quick and easy to read.

❑ There are no misspellings, grammatical errors, or other mistakes.

Tip
SUGGESTIONS Show your letter to friends and people you respect, then evaluate their feedback and make adjustments appropriately. The ultimate test, however, for whether you have a good cover letter is to send it to employers. If it gets you job interviews, you have a great letter!

Hot Off the Press

Ready for a big ego boost? One of the most satisfying parts of this marketing project is seeing your letter all formatted and produced on nice paper. Let's talk about how to get your letter into ship shape and ready to set sail.

The Nuts and Bolts of Typing This Thing

If possible, create your letter using a computer and print it out on a quality printer (laser, ink jet, or the like). Avoid using a dot-matrix printer—you'd be better off using an electric typewriter.

Before printing it out, be sure that your letter is centered on the page and the spacing is consistent between paragraphs and between sections (date, heading, salutation, body, closing, enclosure).

Print, Points, and Other Particulars

There are two categories of type (also referred to as *font*): serif and sans serif.

- Serif font

    Serif font can be identified by the little feet that appear on each letter. Three popular serif fonts are Palatino, Times Roman, and Bookman. The text of this bullet point is printed in Times Roman.

- Sans serif font

    Sans serif characters do not have little feet on them. Helvetica, Avant Garde, and Chicago are three commonly used sans serif fonts. Helvetica is used in this bullet point.

Either a serif or sans serif font is permissible for your cover letter, however, most graphic design professionals contend that serif type is easier to read. For that reason, most of the sample letters in this book use a serif font.

Font size is measured by *points*—the larger the point number, the larger the size of the character. Your computer word processing program will allow you to determine the point size of the font you choose. I recommend using 12-point type (no smaller) for your cover letter so that it can be read easily. An 11-point font is acceptable for your resume if it is formatted with bullet point statements, but a letter that is printed in less than 12-point type becomes hard to read because of its paragraph format.

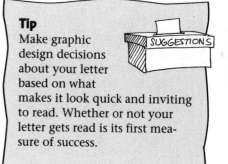

Rule

Rule #4: Make It Quick and Easy to Read. You can make your cover letter easy to read by avoiding excessive use of italics in your text.

Tip

Make graphic design decisions about your letter based on what makes it look quick and inviting to read. Whether or not your letter gets read is its first measure of success.

Q & A

Is it alright to mix fonts within my cover letter?

Usually one does not mix fonts within a document, however, some find that using a sans serif font for a bold title such as your name in your letterhead and a serif font for the text can lend graphic appeal.

Looking Classy on Paper

Select paper that's appropriate for the type of work you're going after. It makes sense that someone going for an executive management position is going to have higher-end paper than someone seeking a clerical position. I personally don't like fancy textured or "parchment" sheets—they look pretentious. I like good old plain white that has just a little more weight than the standard 20-lb. paper used for copying. That extra weight sends a subconscious message of quality to the reader without screaming out, "This paper cost big bucks!"

What about paper color? There are two schools of thought on using colored paper as the backdrop for your cover letter.

➤ Thumbs down on colored paper. White paper yields the highest contrast with your black print—high contrast helps create clear reproductions when your letter is faxed and photocopied.

➤ Thumbs up on colored paper. Colored paper can make your letter stand out on an employer's desk, since most of your competitors will have used white paper. If you decide to take the look-at-me colored paper approach, heed this warning: Use very light tones (gray, buff, blue, or pink). Hot pinks and the like just don't cut it with most employers.

> **Watch Out!**
> CAUTION Typos in a cover letter are deadly! Make sure yours is typo-free by using your spell checker (if you're working on a computer), proofreading thoroughly, and asking someone else to check it once more. Pay particular attention to the names of the employer and the company!

One administrative assistant pointed out to me, "When the paper is too thick, it jams up the copier. That makes me mad and I'm apt to throw the sheet away." Oops! Better not get on the wrong side of an administrative assistant who, at that moment, wields the fate of your career. Solution: Choose something a little heavier than 20-lb. but not as thick as card stock.

Signing Your Life Away

Before you stuff your cover letter and resume into an envelope and rush out the door to the nearest mailbox, don't forget your John Hancock. Ah yes, the final personal touch to your masterpiece is your signature.

You've left about four spaces between your complimentary close and your printed name—that's where you sign your name (see Chapter 5, "Step One—Set the Stage," for details on the layout for the letter format you've chosen). Use a pen or narrow felt-tip marker with blue or black ink.

You may sign either your first and last name (middle initial is optional), or if your letter has had an especially personal, friendly tone, it might be a nice touch to sign just your first name. The typed version of your name that appears just below your sign be your *full* name.

A Word About Resumes

Now that you have a dynamite cover letter, you need an explosive resume to match it! In a nutshell, here are five points to keep in mind while creating your resume.

> ➤ Your resume is a marketing piece about your future (your next job), not a grim confessional about your past.

> ➤ Write about achievements instead of lifeless job descriptions so that the employer will know that you are *good* at what you do.

> ➤ Since your resume suggests to an employer what you want in your next job description, only write about experiences that you liked and want to repeat.

> ➤ Do not use paragraph formatting in your resume—use bullet point statements so that your marketing piece looks quick and easy to read.

> ➤ Don't lie. You don't have to disclose all information, but everything that appears on your resume must be true.

Q & A

How many pages should my resume be?

Your resume should be no more than two pages long. If you can create a one-pager, all the better, as long as the print is large enough and there is enough white space on the page to make it look inviting to read.

If your resume doesn't measure up to all five of the above notes, I suggest you go back to the resume drawing board. My book, *The Complete Idiot's Guide to the Perfect Resume*, can help by leading you through its straight-forward, nine-step process.

Envelope Stuffer Alert!

Instead of squishing your letter and resume into the standard 4 × 9-inch business envelope, mail your marketing duo in a large 9 × 12-inch envelope. In the larger envelope, your documents will lie flat, allowing them to arrive without creases that crack the print. In that way, they'll make nice clear reproductions when slipped into the employer's copy machine.

Tip
Don't staple your cover letter and resume together. Paper-clip them together instead.

SUGGESTIONS

147

Q & A

My printer won't accept a 9 × 12-inch envelope. Is it acceptable to address it by hand?

It's perfectly fine to hand address your envelope. Another option is to type or print out a plain white label if you have sticky labels for a typewriter or computer printer.

Just-In-Time Delivery

You've finished writing and producing your letter. It looks and sounds great. Now what? You need to get it into the hands of your potential employer. Read on for some ways you can get your job search tools delivered on time.

Doing the Snail Mail Crawl

If you're not facing an immediate application deadline, the good old U.S. Postal Service (sometimes referred to as snail mail) will probably do just fine for sending your resume and cover letter. There's no need to send your packet certified or registered, just put a stamp for first class delivery on the envelope and drop it in a nearby mail slot.

Pony Express

You're in a hurry to get your resume and cover letter to an employer—and you want it to get noticed when it arrives—so you turn to one of the overnight or two-day courier services such as FedEx, UPS, or the U.S. Postal Service. Many of these services will pick up your packet at your address, or you can take your bundle of goodies to their dispatch center and have it sent from there.

Here's how to prepare your packet.

1. Print out your cover letter and resume.
2. Place your material in a flat envelope with the employer's name and address on it (just in case your stuff wiggles out of the courier's packaging).
3. Hand it to the courier and he will put it into a cardboard envelope for delivery.
4. Fill out the courier's form and pay him his fee.

Q & A

What's an appropriate follow-up schedule after sending a resume?

Calculate the amount of time needed (depending on whether you send it via U.S. mail, courier, fax, or electronic mail) for your resume and cover letter to arrive. Make your follow-up call *one day after* you think your packet has landed on the employer's desk. Keep in mind that in larger corporations there often can be 1–2 days needed for internal sorting and routing of mail.

Your Job Is Just a Fax Away

There are two reasons why you may want to fax your cover letter and resume to a company:

➤ To meet a tight deadline, or

➤ The job posting says, "Please fax resume"

The cover letter and resume that you fax should be created exactly as the one you would send through the U.S. mail. Since the two are being sent through the wondrous fax machine, they should be accompanied by a fax cover sheet.

Produce a simple cover sheet that states:

1. The date
2. To whom the fax is being sent
3. Who is sending the fax (that's you!)
4. The total number of pages being faxed and the general contents of those sheets

A typical fax cover sheet looks something like this:

Date: September 13, 1997

To: Brad Thompson

From: Susan Ireland

Pages: Three—cover letter

                  resume

                  cover sheet

Q & A

If I fax my cover letter and resume, should I also mail them to the employer?

Call the employer and ask this question of him. Some companies prefer not to receive a duplicate in the mail, simply because they are so inundated with paperwork as it is. Others would appreciate having the "real thing" sent on nice paper for their permanent files. If you're unable to contact the employer to ask this question, go ahead and send a duplicate in the mail, being sure to state in your cover letter that it is a follow-up to the fax you sent a few days earlier.

Watch Out!

CAUTION The formatting (indents, bold type, etc.) of your letter and resume may get lost in the electronic transmission, especially if you're e-mailing from one on-line provider to another. To reduce the risk of this happening, use simple formatting in your documents (for your cover letter, that might mean using the block format described in Chapter 5, "Step One—Set the Stage"). Once your material is e-mailed, inquire of the employer if your documents arrived in good shape.

Rule

Rule #2: Show Personality. A memo format allows you to use a more familiar tone since it's clear that you work under the same roof as the hiring manager.

E-mail: High Speed Communication

If your potential employer is expecting your resume and cover letter to arrive by e-mail, you need two things in order to comply:

➤ The employer's e-mail address, and

➤ Access to a computer that has on-line capabilities.

If you don't have an on-line setup yourself, you can gain on-line access through computers at some libraries, career centers, employment agencies, and copy centers.

Sending e-mail is a cinch, even if you've never done it before. If you're unfamiliar with the procedure, ask someone knowledgeable to help you, or read the e-mail instructions for the particular on-line service you are using.

Dear Boss, Internally Yours

What if you're applying for a promotion within the company where you currently work? I suggest that you attach a memo to your resume instead of using the official cover letter format. A memo clipped to your resume immediately identifies your application as one coming from within the company (which is frequently an employer's preferred source of recruitment).

The Rules of the Road and all the steps for creating a good cover letter from Parts 1 and 2 apply to your memo. The only difference is the format of your communication. It might look something like the following:

DESKTOP INFORMATION SYSTEMS

MEMO

TO: Ray Marquez, DIS Telephone Services Manager

FROM: Matt Clemons, Information Specialist *MC*

DATE: May 9, 199X

RE: Telephone Services Supervisor position

> Matt sends a friendly, informal message to a supervisor he has known for years.

Ray, I want to throw in my hat for the DIS Supervisor position. I believe this promotion would be a natural step for me, as I have already taken on many supervisory-type functions on my own initiative.

A brief recap of some of my achievements over the past three years:

* By completely re-vamping our referral database, I ensured that our information is complete, accurate and up-to-date.
* I increased DIS visibility and credibility in the community by participating in outreach efforts, including conferences and job fairs.
* I earned team members' confidence, frequently assisting co-workers with their calls.

I'm aware that it can be tricky to "promote from within," but I can honestly say I believe I have the support of the entire DIS team in seeking this position.

Thanks for considering my candidacy. I'll check with you next week about the interview schedule.

> Even though the reader knows Matt's a good worker, Matt reminds him of specific achievements.

The Least You Need to Know

➤ Go over the Top Ten List to double-check that you did everything you were supposed to do on your cover letter.

➤ Produce your letter on a quality printer or electric typewriter, using appropriate paper.

➤ Sign your name just below the complimentary close of your letter, using blue or black ink.

➤ Use a 9 × 12-inch envelope to mail your material so that it arrives without fold marks.

➤ Substitute a memo format for the traditional letter format when applying to your current employer for a promotion.

Chapter 11

Recycling Your Cover Letter

In This Chapter

➤ Evaluating the response from your first cover letter

➤ Developing a plan for sending out more cover letters and resumes

➤ Revising your original cover letter to apply to other employers

➤ Ensuring that future versions of your message don't sound like form letters

Now that you have one cover letter out the door, you may want to apply to other employers. After all, you probably don't want to have all your eggs in one basket. Does that mean you have to begin all over again at Chapter 1 to create your second, third, and twentieth cover letters?

No, you don't have to go back to the beginning. Having gone through the cover letter writing steps in Parts 1 and 2, you have a good start on your subsequent versions. This chapter will look at how you can revise your first cover letter to use for other job applications.

Wow, That Was a Lot of Work the First Time Around

Yes, you worked hard creating your first cover letter. From here on, cover letter writing will be a lot easier because you have a good model (your first cover letter) to springboard off of. I'm going to show you how to identify and recycle the winning aspects of the letter you penned using the first half of this book.

Q & A

Should I make a generic cover letter and then change the name in the salutation for each employer?

I don't recommend that tactic. A generic letter will sound like a form letter, and an employer will identify it as such. A better approach is to start with a strong cover letter that you've tailored to your first choice employer. Then revise that letter, using the steps presented in this chapter.

Sizing Up the Response—Good and Bad

First, you need to evaluate the performance of your original cover letter. Ask yourself what worked and what didn't work. Let me help you figure out the answers to those questions.

What Worked?

What positive response did you get from the employer about your cover letter, even if you didn't get the interview or the job?

➤ If the hiring manager mentioned that she liked your clean, inviting presentation of information—bravo on your formatting! Employ the same easy-to-read layout in your next letter.

➤ Maybe she appreciated the contents of your letter since it pointed out how you fit into her company. Good going! Use a similar technique in future versions of your letter.

Did you achieve the action you desired as a result of your letter?

➤ Your closing line worked if the employer invited you for an interview, even though you were unable to follow up on your letter by phone. It sounds like your closing line was a good instigator of action—perhaps one you can use in other letters when you are unable to call the employer.

➤ Maybe your reader was poised and ready to invite you for an interview when you made your follow-up call to him, as you mentioned you would in your letter. Cool! Your ambitious approach will probably work in other cover letters.

What interview questions did your cover letter stimulate?

➤ Maybe the interviewer picked up on the personal connection you mentioned in your letter, adding a comfortable air to the interview. A good trick to duplicate in your next letter.

➤ Perhaps the conversation focused on your strengths and qualifications for the job—just as you listed in your cover letter. Good show! Repeat that "list" concept in your next cover letter.

All these winning points of your first letter can be repeated in other cover letters you prepare. So, refer to this list while writing subsequent letters, and... keep up the good work!

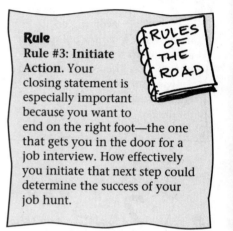

Rule

Rule #3: Initiate Action. Your closing statement is especially important because you want to end on the right foot—the one that gets you in the door for a job interview. How effectively you initiate that next step could determine the success of your job hunt.

What Didn't Work?

Did you not hear from the employer after sending your cover letter and resume? If not, why?

➤ Maybe your packet never got to its destination. Call the company to see if it arrived. If it got lost, offer to fax your material right away. (Read Chapter 10, "Wrap It Up," to learn how to fax your information to an employer.)

➤ If you didn't use a forceful close in your letter, you probably lost out to a more assertive applicant. In your next letter, initiate action by telling the reader that you will call or drop by to arrange for an interview. Chapter 8, "Step Four—Closing the Sale," explains how to write dynamite closers.

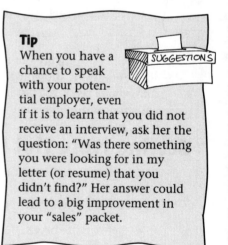

Tip

When you have a chance to speak with your potential employer, even if it is to learn that you did not receive an interview, ask her the question: "Was there something you were looking for in my letter (or resume) that you didn't find?" Her answer could lead to a big improvement in your "sales" packet.

Did you get a flat "no" in response to your request for a job interview? If so, why?

➤ If you forgot to say that you possess the requirements for the job, be sure to announce your relevant qualifications in your next letter.

➤ Maybe you were too modest when presenting your skills and experience. In that case, you need to beef up your sales pitch in your next round.

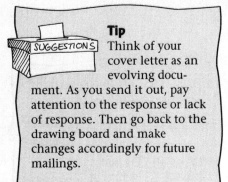

Tip

Think of your cover letter as an evolving document. As you send it out, pay attention to the response or lack of response. Then go back to the drawing board and make changes accordingly for future mailings.

Did you get invited for an interview for a job you didn't want? If so, why?

➤ If you didn't state a job objective in your cover letter and resume, that could be why the employer didn't consider you for the right type of work. Be sure to have a job objective statement in your letter and resume for all future job requests.

➤ Your job objective might have been unrealistically high for you at this point in your career. If so, set your job target a little lower for your next application.

Q & A

Won't a job objective statement in my cover letter limit my possibilities for employment?

Having a job objective statement in your letter will not deter an employer from considering you for positions other than the one you suggest.

Do your best to figure out how you can improve your letter writing by asking yourself the above questions and going over the four letter-writing steps in Part 2. Once you've done that, you're ready to start investigating more job leads so you can hit the streets again with your self-marketing materials.

Scoring More Hot Leads

Before you can write your next cover letter, you need to decide to whom you want to apply for a job. That means you have to investigate your job market and discover some hot leads. I suggest that you:

➤ Network, network, network

➤ Brainstorm about companies you'd love to work for

➤ Check out job hotlines

➤ Do some on-line detective work

➤ Contact a recruiter

➤ Check the "help wanted" ads in the newspaper

Here are some tips for each of the above suggestions.

A Friend to Lean On

Networking among friends, family, business associates, and people with influence in your field is the most valuable means of learning about job opportunities. Be sure to contact everyone you know who might be aware of a hiring manager to whom you can send a cover letter and resume.

Companies to Die For

You may have a company in mind that you would love to work for. Even without knowing if there are any job openings, you can contact human resources or the manager of the department you're interested in, using a letter and resume that clearly indicates your marketable skills.

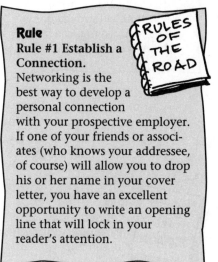

Rule
Rule #1 Establish a Connection. Networking is the best way to develop a personal connection with your prospective employer. If one of your friends or associates (who knows your addressee, of course) will allow you to drop his or her name in your cover letter, you have an excellent opportunity to write an opening line that will lock in your reader's attention.

Lists and Lists of Jobs

Many career centers, state agencies, and nonprofit organizations have on-site job listings and telephone job hotlines. Some organizations charge a fee for using them. Others may ask you to do volunteer work to "pay" for the services they provide. To find such organizations, look in the Yellow Pages under employment-related headings such as "career centers," where you should find private, nonprofit, and state-run agencies.

Jump On-line—Jump on the Job

On the Internet, you can post your cover letter and resume in databases for thousands of employers to see. To find on-line resume banks, conduct a search using job-related terms like "employment," "jobs," "career," "resumes," etc. A good starting point for your on-line hunt is a World Wide Web site called Riley Guide (http://www.jobtrak.com/jobguide/).

Getting Help From the Pros

Collaborating with a recruiter is usually a free and painless way to submit your resume to employers. Recruiters usually specialize according to industry (for example, computer or pharmaceuticals) or profession (for example, sales or executive management). When

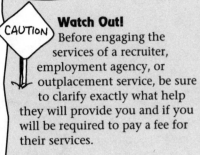

Watch Out!
Before engaging the services of a recruiter, employment agency, or outplacement service, be sure to clarify exactly what help they will provide you and if you will be required to pay a fee for their services.

sending your resume to a recruiter, it should be accompanied by a cover letter that is just as carefully created as one you would send to an employer.

Finding a recruiter can be done by looking in the Yellow Pages under job-related headings such as "Employment Agencies" and by asking career counselors who work in your field.

Keeping Up on the News

Although "help wanted" ads are considered by many to be the least effective place to land a job, don't exclude them from your strategy. Many reputable companies use the classified ads as a successful recruiting method. A well-written resume accompanied by a cover letter can grab the reader's eye and secure an interview, despite the overwhelming amount of competition that newspaper ads generate.

Rule
Rule #2: Show **Personality.** By researching your potential employer, you're apt to learn enough to at least *speculate* about your prospective boss' personality. Imagining what she's like will help you write a letter that shows your own character.

Now That You're a Research Expert

Once you've decided to whom you are applying for a job, you're ready to do a little research about the company. To make your cover letter truly effective, you need to know the name of the person to whom you are addressing your letter, as well as a little bit about him or her. Review Chapter 3, "Research Smarts," and then compile the company and manager profiles for your new addressee, along with the "To Say" list described in that chapter. Having made your lists, it's time for the next step in your letter-rewriting process.

Remodeling a Good Thing

OK, you're ready to roll up your sleeves and work on your next letter. Boot up your computer and make a copy of your first cover letter. Working inside the copy (thereby saving your original letter), start at the top and move through the text, customizing it for employer #2.

A Few Tweaks Here and There

Take the following steps, referring to the noted chapters when necessary:

➤ Adjust the date, if necessary. (See Chapter 5, "Step One—Set the Stage.")

➤ Change the inside address and salutation to represent your new addressee. (See Chapter 5, "Step One—Set the Stage.")

➤ Determine what tone you want your communication to have, and adjust the language of your new letter accordingly. (See Chapter 6, "Step Two—Follow My Lead.") For example:

Since you originally met employer #1 at a football game, you started your letter to him with the playful opener, "How 'bout those 49ers last Sunday!" Your research tells you that employer #2 is a pretty traditional fellow, so your letter to him starts with the more conservative line: "I enjoyed meeting you at the sports conference last Monday."

Q & A

How freely should I express my personality in my cover letter?

Be as friendly and familiar as you feel is appropriate, given how well you know the person. The operative word is "appropriate." To a large extent, you must rely on your common sense and intuition, just as you do when you meet someone in 3-D.

➤ Establish a personal connection with your new prospective employer using names, situations, or interests common to your current reader. (See Chapter 6, "Step Two—Follow My Lead.") For example:

In your letter to employer #1, you may have introduced yourself as his sister's former supervisor. When writing to employer #2, you might remind him that you and he met over a game of tennis last spring.

➤ Replace or eliminate any particulars in the text that refer specifically to the addressee of your first cover letter. (See Chapter 7, "Step Three—The Pitch.") For example:

Your first letter might have referred to employer #1's business goals. In your new letter, change that statement to reflect employer #2's goals.

➤ Present your selling points so that your new reader will identify you as a wise investment. (See Chapter 7, "Step Three—The Pitch.") For example:

You marketed your sales and supervisory skills to employer #1. Employer #2 might be more interested in your writing and training skills.

➤ Initiate action in the closing paragraph according whether or not you're able to telephone your new reader. (See Chapter 8, "Step Four—Closing the Sale.") For example:

In your letter to employer #1, you said that you would call him to set up an interview appointment. But employer #2's ad specifically states, "no phone calls." Therefore, you could create an incentive for him to call you by saying that next week you will be on vacation and available for an interview.

To further demonstrate the above points, I've included the following two letters, both written by Cynthia Roberts. Cynthia's letter to Hank Stearn was a revision of her letter to Linda Shankin.

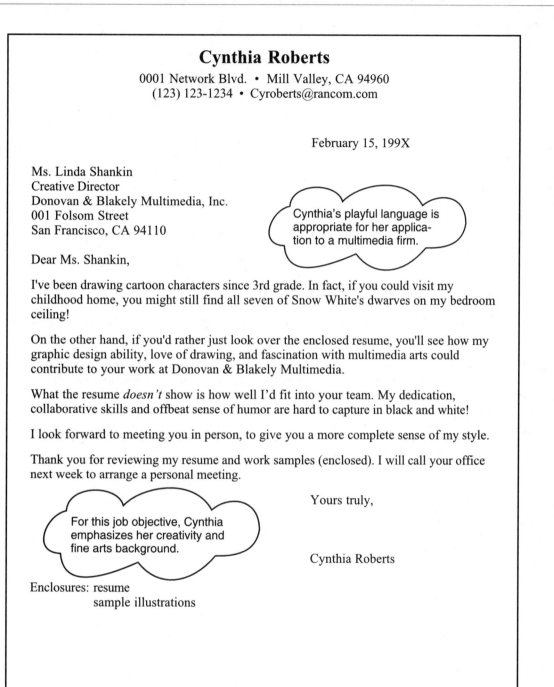

Cynthia Roberts

0001 Network Blvd. • Mill Valley, CA 94960
(123) 123-1234 • Cyroberts@rancom.com

February 15, 199X

Ms. Linda Shankin
Creative Director
Donovan & Blakely Multimedia, Inc.
001 Folsom Street
San Francisco, CA 94110

Dear Ms. Shankin,

I've been drawing cartoon characters since 3rd grade. In fact, if you could visit my childhood home, you might still find all seven of Snow White's dwarves on my bedroom ceiling!

On the other hand, if you'd rather just look over the enclosed resume, you'll see how my graphic design ability, love of drawing, and fascination with multimedia arts could contribute to your work at Donovan & Blakely Multimedia.

What the resume *doesn't* show is how well I'd fit into your team. My dedication, collaborative skills and offbeat sense of humor are hard to capture in black and white!

I look forward to meeting you in person, to give you a more complete sense of my style.

Thank you for reviewing my resume and work samples (enclosed). I will call your office next week to arrange a personal meeting.

Yours truly,

Cynthia Roberts

Enclosures: resume
            sample illustrations

Cynthia's playful language is appropriate for her application to a multimedia firm.

For this job objective, Cynthia emphasizes her creativity and fine arts background.

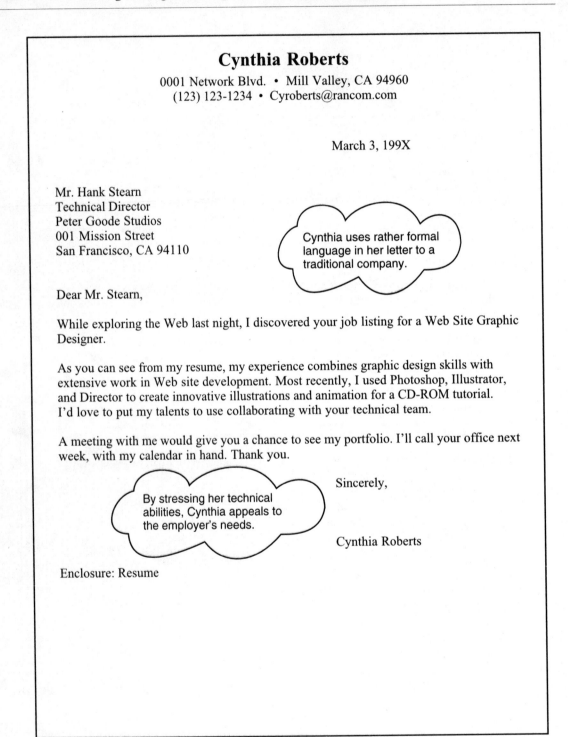

Cynthia Roberts

0001 Network Blvd. • Mill Valley, CA 94960
(123) 123-1234 • Cyroberts@rancom.com

March 3, 199X

Mr. Hank Stearn
Technical Director
Peter Goode Studios
001 Mission Street
San Francisco, CA 94110

> Cynthia uses rather formal language in her letter to a traditional company.

Dear Mr. Stearn,

While exploring the Web last night, I discovered your job listing for a Web Site Graphic Designer.

As you can see from my resume, my experience combines graphic design skills with extensive work in Web site development. Most recently, I used Photoshop, Illustrator, and Director to create innovative illustrations and animation for a CD-ROM tutorial. I'd love to put my talents to use collaborating with your technical team.

A meeting with me would give you a chance to see my portfolio. I'll call your office next week, with my calendar in hand. Thank you.

> By stressing her technical abilities, Cynthia appeals to the employer's needs.

Sincerely,

Cynthia Roberts

Enclosure: Resume

Ready to Go

There you have it: the second generation of your cover letter. And you can generate a countless number of spin-offs. As long as you use the four "Rules of the Road" (see Chapter 2, "Winning Concepts") for each version, your cover letters will never sound like form letters, no matter how many you write. That's the art of effective cover letter writing.

The Least You Need to Know

➤ Before creating your second cover letter, make a list of what worked and what didn't work with your first one.

➤ Decide to whom you want to send your next job application by networking, brainstorming about desirable companies, checking on-line, talking to recruiters, and digging through your newspaper's classified ads.

➤ Customize your original cover letter to make it a strong sales pitch for your new reader—employer #2.

➤ Be sure that your letter doesn't sound like a form letter by following the guidelines in Parts 1 and 2.

Part 4
Other Hardworking Letters

Close your eyes and imagine the following...

You've written an invitation to a stranger that leads to breakthroughs in your career change—or saves you months or years on a job you would have hated.

You've penned a one-page letter that, on its own, yields three payoffs: an interview for the job of your dreams; an interview agenda that spotlights your value; and a powerful kick-off to high salary negotiations.

You've whipped out a very short thank-you note to a hiring manager that turns the tide—in your favor, of course—after your job interview!

These letters don't have to stay in your imagination. Friendly, persuasive letters that dare to ask for what you want—that's what Part 4 is about. Can these "extra" letters (broadcast letters, informational interview requests, and thank-you notes) really make a difference in winning a job? You bet they can! And they can reap big rewards... for you!

Chapter 12

Announcing, Announcing: Broadcast Letters

In This Chapter

➤ What is a broadcast letter and how will it expedite your job search?

➤ Targeting a particular employer with a broadcast letter

➤ Designing a strategy for a mass mailing

➤ Graphic elements of a compelling broadcast letter

➤ Capitalizing on the broadcast letter's main feature: achievement statements

➤ Producing your letter and getting it into the employer's hands

The broadcast letter is one of the most daring written methods to apply for a job. It's an untraditional approach, and, as I mentioned in Chapter 1, "You Gotta Have a Strategy," one that can make an outstanding impression on an open-minded employer.

This chapter takes you by the hand through the steps of developing your broadcast letter. It also teaches you how to figure out what your relevant achievements are and how to put them in your broadcast letter so you get the most out of every word.

What Is a Broadcast Letter, Anyway?

A broadcast letter is a hybrid between a resume and a cover letter. The two are rolled into one to become a super sales letter that, on its own, opens the door for a job interview.

Wow! That's expecting a lot from a single piece of paper. Yes, and the broadcast letter measures up to the task. It uses all the marketing techniques of a cover letter (see Part 2, "Your Resume Booster"), with special emphasis on achievement statements in the body of the letter (just like a resume). And to make the achievement lines stand out, you can format them with bullet points, making your broadcast letter even *look* a little like a resume.

Q & A

Can I write one generic broadcast letter to cover three different job objectives?

If you have several job objectives in mind, you will probably need to use a job search strategy that involves multiple versions of your broadcast letter—one for each job objective.

Want to see what a broadcast letter looks like? Check out this one coming up by Esther Dixon.

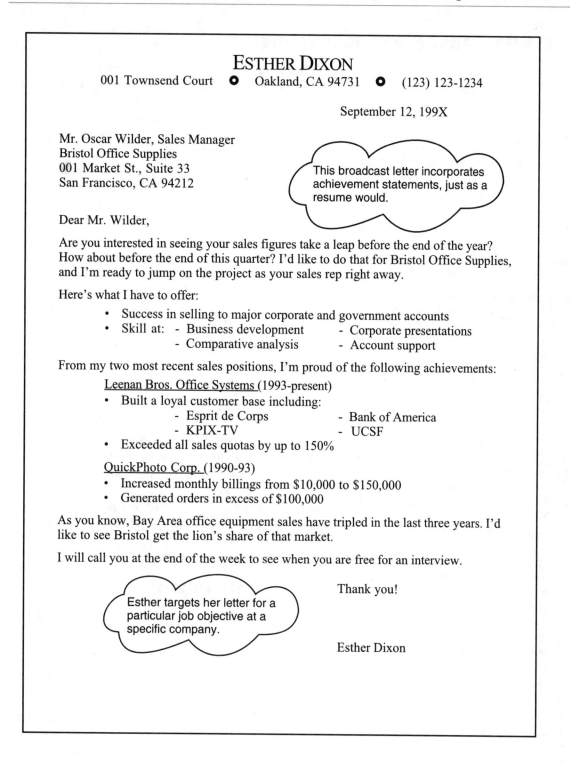

ESTHER DIXON

001 Townsend Court ● Oakland, CA 94731 ● (123) 123-1234

September 12, 199X

Mr. Oscar Wilder, Sales Manager
Bristol Office Supplies
001 Market St., Suite 33
San Francisco, CA 94212

This broadcast letter incorporates achievement statements, just as a resume would.

Dear Mr. Wilder,

Are you interested in seeing your sales figures take a leap before the end of the year? How about before the end of this quarter? I'd like to do that for Bristol Office Supplies, and I'm ready to jump on the project as your sales rep right away.

Here's what I have to offer:

- Success in selling to major corporate and government accounts
- Skill at: - Business development   - Corporate presentations
           - Comparative analysis   - Account support

From my two most recent sales positions, I'm proud of the following achievements:

Leenan Bros. Office Systems (1993-present)
- Built a loyal customer base including:
                - Esprit de Corps   - Bank of America
                - KPIX-TV   - UCSF
- Exceeded all sales quotas by up to 150%

QuickPhoto Corp. (1990-93)
- Increased monthly billings from $10,000 to $150,000
- Generated orders in excess of $100,000

As you know, Bay Area office equipment sales have tripled in the last three years. I'd like to see Bristol get the lion's share of that market.

I will call you at the end of the week to see when you are free for an interview.

Thank you!

Esther targets her letter for a particular job objective at a specific company.

Esther Dixon

A Sales Letter About Your Future

Tip
Your broadcast letter should so strongly paint the picture of you at your next job that there appears to be little or no transition into your new job—even if you're making a big career change.

Tip
A broadcast letter is sometimes the perfect document when applying to an employer you know personally. It gives more information than the typical letter, yet isn't as formal as a resume.

Rule
Rule #4: Make It Quick and Easy to Read. Think of your broadcast letter as a valuable piece of real estate in Manhattan where every increment of space should be capitalized. As land is used for buildings, signs, and pathways, use the space on your broadcast letter for short paragraphs, bullet statements, and lists. And just as landscaping and parks are appreciated in congested urban areas, white space gives relief to your reader's eye.

The secret to getting a new and exciting job is to write your broadcast letter from the perspective that it's a *sales* letter. In other words, sift through all the experience, skills, and personal attributes you have and select only the juiciest, most *relevant* achievements that effectively say, "I'm the best person for the job."

The operative word here is "relevant." Don't try to tell your whole life story. Present only what paints the picture of you at your next job. That's right, your letter is a word-picture of your future.

Here's how to create a broadcast letter that leads the reader to envision you at your next job: Imagine that you're an artist with an empty canvas (such as your computer screen or blank sheet of paper) in front of you. Your assignment is to paint a picture of yourself at your next job, using any of the following four tools:

➤ Your experience (such as previous job titles, volunteer work, or school projects)

➤ Your skill areas (such as management, computer knowledge, or sales)

➤ Your concerns (such as the environment, homelessness, or human rights)

➤ Your personality (such as dependability, sense of humor, or ability to communicate)

If you follow this advice, here's what will happen when the employer reads your letter: She'll find herself imagining you working for her. And that's what will make her want to call you for an interview.

No Long Paragraphs!

Dense paragraphs in your broadcast letter will discourage a busy manager from reading your letter. Many poorly constructed broadcast letters have long paragraphs, undoubtedly filled with juicy information. The problem is, nobody wants to read a long paragraph when they're in a hurry. A dense paragraph demands too much time to read.

Here's the remedy to the long paragraph dilemma: Create short paragraphs and use bullet points to break your material into bite-sized pieces. A bullet statement effectively says, "Here's an independent thought that's quick and easy to read."

Straight Shooting: Bullet Statements

For the best effect, start each accomplishment statement on a new line so that all the bullet points line up on the left, like this:

- Organized exhibition openings at the Circle Gallery, attended by as many as 200 collectors and well-known artists.
- Assisted the event planner of Art Against Homelessness, an art auction that raised $75,000 for homeless-related charities.
- Managed location and entertainment for a celebrity event that raised more than $25,000 for OSIN.

Step One—Down to Basics

The first step is an easy one: getting your heading and introductory information on your page. There are two ways to set up your information, so follow the directions below for the type of mailing you are conducting: individual or group.

To Someone Special

For a broadcast letter being sent to a particular employer, use the following guidelines to create the heading, date, inside address, and salutation of your letter, referring to Chapter 5, "Step One—Set the Stage," when necessary.

1. Construct the letterhead (your name, address, and contact information) at the top of your page.
2. Select a letter style (block, semiblock, full block, or simplified) from the templates in Chapter 5.
3. A few spaces down from your letterhead, place today's date according to the style of letter you chose.
4. The employer's name should appear in the inside address and salutation, just as it would if you were writing a cover letter.

Take a look at the following broadcast letter by Dave Berwick, which was designed for an individual employer.

Watch Out!
CAUTION
Don't substitute an asterisk (*) for a bullet point. An asterisk tells the reader to look below for a footnote. That's not what you mean!

Rule
RULES OF THE ROAD
Rule #4: Make It Quick and Easy to Read. Your broadcast letter may get only about *eight seconds* to win your prospective employer's approval. In that initial quick scan, your reader will determine if your letter warrants serious review. So use smart graphic design and strict editing to make your most striking and relevant accomplishments jump out at her during her first glance.

DAVE BERWICK
0010 Lindsay Avenue • Albany, NY 23907 • (123) 123-1234

July 15, 199X

Ms. Genine Wilson
Marketing Director
HomeCare HMO, Inc.
001 Forest Hills Station
Lancaster, MA 04221

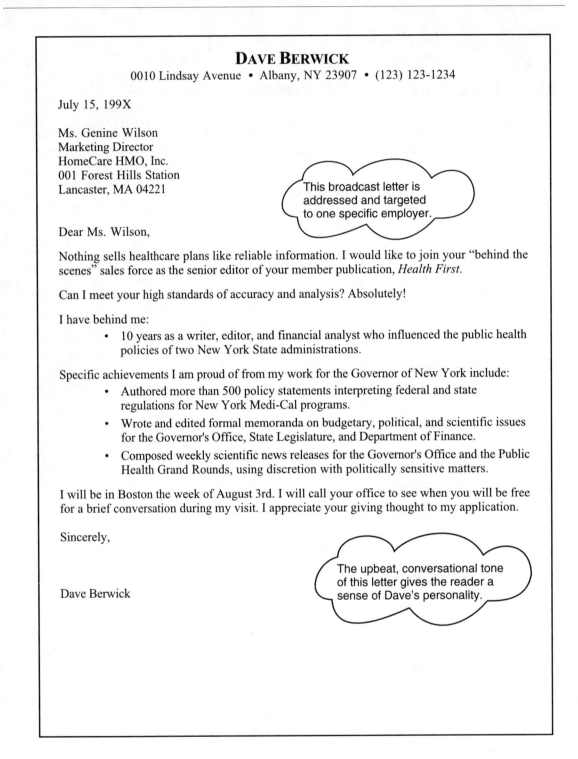

This broadcast letter is addressed and targeted to one specific employer.

Dear Ms. Wilson,

Nothing sells healthcare plans like reliable information. I would like to join your "behind the scenes" sales force as the senior editor of your member publication, *Health First*.

Can I meet your high standards of accuracy and analysis? Absolutely!

I have behind me:

- 10 years as a writer, editor, and financial analyst who influenced the public health policies of two New York State administrations.

Specific achievements I am proud of from my work for the Governor of New York include:

- Authored more than 500 policy statements interpreting federal and state regulations for New York Medi-Cal programs.
- Wrote and edited formal memoranda on budgetary, political, and scientific issues for the Governor's Office, State Legislature, and Department of Finance.
- Composed weekly scientific news releases for the Governor's Office and the Public Health Grand Rounds, using discretion with politically sensitive matters.

I will be in Boston the week of August 3rd. I will call your office to see when you will be free for a brief conversation during my visit. I appreciate your giving thought to my application.

Sincerely,

The upbeat, conversational tone of this letter gives the reader a sense of Dave's personality.

Dave Berwick

A Group Announcement

For a mass mailing, be straightforward about the fact that you're sending the same letter to many recipients. After all, there's nothing shameful about conducting a large mailing for a job hunt—especially if you're up-front about it.

Here's how to indicate that you're orchestrating a mass mailing, without losing impact. Take the steps mentioned earlier for a broadcast letter going to a particular employer, except for the following:

1. Don't put an inside address on your broadcast letter. A little below your letterhead, place the date, and then move right on to the salutation.

2. Use a salutation that acknowledges that you are sending this letter to many people. For example:

    Dear Prospective Employer,

    Dear Hiring Manager,

    If you feel daring, try something like:

    Greetings from the Job Hunt Field!

    For Managers Looking for a Top Salesperson,

The next mass mailing piece by Hank Tilden incorporates the above points. The language effectively tells the reader that the letter is part of a large mailing.

Watch Out!

Don't insert the reader's name into your mass-mailed letter with the idea that it will trick the reader into thinking your letter was sent only to him. How many times have *you* gotten junk mail with your name in the salutation of the letter? One look at junk mail like that and you immediately recognize that the sender has used the same form letter for a zillion people. Instead, use a salutation that acknowledges that your letter was sent to others also.

Hank Tilden

001 Shore Road - Boston, MA 06839 - (123) 123-1234

August 13, 199X

Hank starts with a splashy heading that announces his job objective.

Product Marketing Professional for Hire!

Business is booming again in the international market. I have some ideas for helping my next employer snatch the market share from the competition.

Please take a moment to read my mini-resume.

Profile
- 10 years as a Product Marketing Professional for some of the most prominent corporations in their industries.
- Strength in creating business strategies that increase perceived product value and capture market share.
- Knowledge of international vendor markets.

Business Accomplishments
- Cut product costs $25 million in one year by identifying key global resources for a $400 million business unit. (Mervyn's)
  Markets: - Asia   - U.S.A.   - Indian Subcontinent
           - Mexico   - Middle East   - South America
- Increased profitability of a $50 million division, through strong budget and inventory management. (The Arrow Company)
- Reduced product development lead time 30% by driving six departments to achieve an aggressive calendar. (Mervyn's)
- Launched a $10 million product line which increased overall customer base approximately 20%. (The Arrow Company)

Dollars are being spent which could be going into your pocket. I can turn that situation around — starting the 1st of September. Please call me at (123) 123-1234 so that we can begin making plans now!

Thank you!

Strong achievements make Hank look valuable.

Hank Tilden

Step Two—Follow the Leader

The lead paragraph is critical! Read Chapter 6, "Step Two—Follow My Lead," to get a handle on how to come up with an opening paragraph that knocks the reader off his feet.

Whether your broadcast letter is targeted to a specific employer or it's slated to be a mass-mailer, any of the three types of lead-in lines (formal, friendly, or bold) spoken about in Chapter 6 will work.

In a broadcast letter, it's especially important to declare your job objective since you are not including a resume with that statement on it. So, close to the beginning of your correspondence, tell your reader what type of work you seek. That way she will know how to interpret the rest of the information you provide.

Step Three—Body Building

The body of the broadcast letter is what differentiates a broadcast from a cover letter. Unlike a cover letter, the broadcast letter absolutely *requires* a special ingredient: dynamite achievement statements! Since the principles for crafting the body of a cover letter will be insightful in writing the body paragraphs in the broadcast letter, review Chapter 7, "Step Three—The Pitch." Then return to this section and read on to learn why achievements are so important and how to compose them.

Achievements Extraordinaire

Most broadcast letters are so dry you'd think you were in the Sahara Desert while reading them. That's because they focus on boring job duties. Although the reader wants to know what you've done, he or she is even more concerned with whether you achieved the desired results on the job.

So it makes sense that in your broadcast letter, you talk about your experience in terms of achievements instead of monotonous job descriptions. Achievements will impress the reader, make your broadcast letter far more interesting to read, and stimulate productive conversation during your interview.

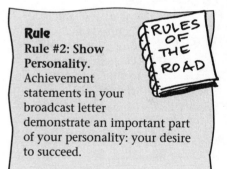

Rule
Rule #2: Show Personality. Achievement statements in your broadcast letter demonstrate an important part of your personality: your desire to succeed.

Make Waves with Dynamite Achievement Statements

By writing about your experience in terms of achievements, not job descriptions, you'll convey three things:

➤ You have the experience and skills to do the job.

➤ You're good at this work and at using these skills.

➤ You like your work. (You must! There's pride in your statements.)

Brain-ticklers

Here are some questions to help you think of relevant achievements for your broadcast letter:

➤ What work-related projects are you proud of that relate to your job objective? For example, "Increased productivity 15 percent as lead engineer on one of Sun Microsystem's development teams."

➤ What are some quantifiable results that point out your ability? For example, "Drove profits from $20 million to $34 million by directing a national celebrity marketing campaign."

➤ When have you demonstrated PAR (Problem, Action, Result)? What was the problem, what was your action to remedy it, and what was the result? For example, "Reduced theft 47 percent by instituting Shoppers' Spy, a tight yet discreet security program."

➤ When did you positively affect the organization, the bottom line, your boss, your coworkers, or your clients? For example, "Enhanced staff morale through a six-month incentive program that also instigated a major increase in sales."

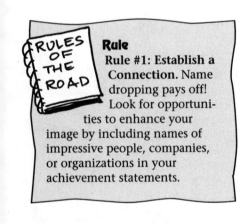

Rule

Rule #1: Establish a Connection. Name dropping pays off! Look for opportunities to enhance your image by including names of impressive people, companies, or organizations in your achievement statements.

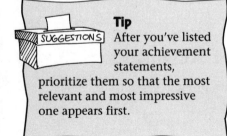

Tip

After you've listed your achievement statements, prioritize them so that the most relevant and most impressive one appears first.

➤ What awards, commendations, publications, etc. have you achieved that relate to your job objective? For example, "Awarded 'Top Salesperson' three consecutive years."

➤ How is success measured in your field? How do you measure up? For example, "Selected by the NIH to represent the United States at the International AIDS Conference in Brazil."

➤ Are you good at using the skills required for this job? When have you demonstrated that to be true? For example, "Used advanced CAD tools to create a totally new look in video game modeling."

➤ What activities, paid and unpaid, have you done that used skills you'll be using at your new job? For example, "Offered academic counseling to 40 students at 'Make It Happen,' a volunteer program at Sanford High School."

➤ When did someone "sit up and take notice" of how skilled you are? For example, "Commended for achieving 97 percent of production goal in an industry where 85 percent is considered high."

Step Four—Closing the Deal

The last paragraph of your broadcast letter is the clincher: You must initiate action. Depending on your broadcast letter's strategy, an active or passive wrap-up line would be appropriate. Let me explain.

The Ball's in Your Court

The best closer is active—one that keeps the ball in your court. In other words, a line that says *you* will call the employer, *you* will stop by to see them, or *you* will in some way take the next step. The active close, of course, works only if you have enough information about the employer to be able to call, drop by, or contact them as you suggest in the closing paragraph.

For tips on how to write a terrific active closer, refer to "Don't Call Me, I'll Call You" in Chapter 8, "Step Four—Closing the Sale." Also, check out the following letter by Terry Powell.

Terry Powell

001 Market St. ◆ Emeryville, CA 94693 ◆ (123) 123-1234

February 18, 199X

Terry uses quotes, achievements, and a strong tone to make a positive impression.

"Money never starts an idea. It is the idea that starts the money." — W.J. Cameron

Does that sound like a great marketing motto? It does to me. That's why my colleagues call me "The Idea Man."

My career took off 13 years ago and hasn't stopped yet:

1990-pres.   BARRY SMITH CLOTHIERS, San Francisco
        Director of Marketing Communications, 1994-pres.
        Director of Public Relations/Licensing Coordinator, 1991-1994
        Public Relations Consultant, 1990

1987-1990   GREY ADVERTISING, INC., New York City
        Creative Services Director

1983-1987   BANANA REPUBLIC, San Francisco
        Media Coordinator

Here are just three out of the many projects I'm proud of from Barry Smith Clothiers:

- Created sales collateral (including videos) and ran the creative portion of the national advertising campaign that established Barry Smith as a manufacturer of quality products.

- Developed and managed a national publicity program that increased retail sales more than 5%, dramatically enhancing brand recognition.

- Authored and designed the first press kit that clearly defined the company's image and product range.

I imagine that we are complementary businessmen: You need marketable ideas; I'm full of them! Shall we talk? I'll give you a call in the next few days to see when we can meet.

Thank you!

Terry makes it clear that she's determined to get an interview.

Terry Powell

Pretty Please?

An alternative to the active close is the passive close. The passive close says essentially: "Please contact me." Although not always as effective as the active line, the passive stance is necessary if:

➤ The employer's identity, address, or phone are unknown and unknowable.

➤ The size of your mass mailing absolutely prohibits you from following up on each letter.

To learn the art of creating a powerful passive close, see "Uh Oh, No Phone Number" in Chapter 8. Then examine the next letter by Patty Graves to see how a passive close can deliver clout from the back seat.

Q & A

Do I need to put "References available upon request" in my broadcast letter?

It's not necessary. Employers know to ask for your references when the time comes (usually after the job interview). Besides, you can use that line in your letter to say something important about why you're qualified for your job objective.

PATTY GRAVES

01 Pine Street, Apt. 31 ◆ San Francisco, CA 94114 ◆ (123) 123-1234

Patty's sales letter appropriately looks and sounds like an advertisement.

January 5, 199X

"I DID IT MY WAY"

Team work never was my thing! No, I've always been a self-motivated, do-it-myself kind of person. That's why I went into commissioned sales 18 years ago, where I've made millions for my employers.

Here's a quick look at what I've done for my most recent boss, Arco:

- Increased premium product sales 10% ($3.5 million) by designing a $2 million advertising and point-of-sale strategy.
- Made winning "sales" presentation regarding a $25 million retail automation project.
- Increased revenue $10 million annually by convincing 7,000 retailers to use electronic funds transfer system.
- Led several testimonial and training presentations that "sold" new technologies to audiences with resistance to change.

I CAN DO IT FOR YOU!

Do you need an independent go-getter like me? If so, we should talk. The sooner I start, the more money I can make for you!

Thank you!

A closing statement that talks money gets employers to call Patty.

Patty Graves

Three, Two, One—Broadcast!

Your masterpiece is completed and it's time to send it on its way. For pointers on the details of choosing paper, signing your name, addressing your envelope, and selecting a delivery method, consult Chapter 10, "Wrap It Up." In addition to the instructions found in that chapter, read below for the type of mailing you are orchestrating.

One-on-One

For an individual mailing, the production process is straightforward. If you're creating your broadcast letter on a computer, print it out on a quality printer (laser, ink jet, or something similar) and it's ready to mail. If you're on a typewriter, your letter will be finished when you make your final pass through the ol' Corona. Whether you're working on a computer or typewriter, follow the guidelines in Chapter 10 for selecting paper for your final draft.

Hear Ye! Hear Ye!

Once you have your master letter for your mass mailing produced on a quality printer or typewriter, it's off to a copy center, unless you have other access to a high quality copier. Don't order a whole slew of copies—start with the number you think you'll need for two weeks of your job search. By copying in short runs, you'll be a lot more inclined to adjust your marketing approach as you pursue your ideal job. That's really important—you need to be prepared to tweak your broadcast letter, if necessary, as you get feedback from employers along the way.

To conduct a mass mailing, you need a qualified, up-to-date mailing list of potential employers. There are several books available that catalog employers by industry and location. You can also hire an information researcher to create a mailing list to your specifications. Locating an information researcher isn't easy. I suggest asking at a career center and looking on-line under career-related subjects to see if one is listed.

When evaluating the results of your mailing, keep in mind that a response of 3 to 4 percent for a commercial direct mailing is considered successful. You can use a similar measuring stick for the effectiveness of your resume mass mailing.

Tip

If you don't have time to do the copying and mailing yourself, you can hire someone else to do it for you. Look in the Yellow Pages under "Secretarial Services," "Word Processing," or "Mailing Services" to find a service that's cost-effective for the size job you have in mind.

The Least You Need to Know

➤ A broadcast letter is a hybrid between a resume and a cover letter. It markets you for the job you want, without using a resume.

➤ To target a particular employer with your broadcast letter, do your research to know her name, job title, and, if possible, her personal and professional style.

➤ Write a broadcast letter for a mass mailing by using speculative company and hiring manager profiles (see Chapter 3, "Research Smarts") to create a generic letter that exudes your personality and intent.

➤ Achievements in the body of your broadcast letter are important. They make your letter scream out: "I've got what it takes…. I've already proven it!"

➤ Ideally, your closing paragraph should take an active approach to initiating the next step. Tell the reader to expect you to call, stop by, or do such-and-such to move the process along.

Chapter 13

Sending an SOS

In This Chapter

➤ Introducing... a special type of interview that gives you inside information about new career possibilities

➤ How to create a letter that asks for an informational interview

➤ Designing a good list of questions to ask your advisor

➤ Follow-up letters that can move you ahead of your competition

---

You want to make a career change, but don't know what you want to do next? You've heard about an occupation that sounds kind of interesting, but you aren't sure exactly what the job entails?

This chapter explains how to write a letter asking for an informational interview, a wonderful method of getting the inside scoop on a profession you are considering.

I Need a Letter to Ask Someone Out to Lunch?

Wouldn't it be nice if you could sit down with someone over a casual lunch and ask them all kinds of questions about what they do for work, precisely because you're wondering whether or not you want to get a job in the same line? That's exactly the type of opportunity I suggest you create. It may not always be over a delicious sandwich—the conversation can take place in an office, park, or company reception area.

Such a meeting is called an *informational interview*. Instead of spending six months on a new job to figure out whether or not it's the career direction you want to take, an informational interview could be a shortcut to that conclusion. It can provide an insider's perspective on:

➤ What skills are required for the job

➤ What advancement possibilities exist

➤ What salary ranges are typical

➤ What industry culture prevails

Discussing the above (and other issues you may have), will help you assess your desire to pursue a new field—without spending a minute on the job. To request an informational interview, you can approach your prospective interviewee by phone, in person, or by letter. I'm going to explain how to ask for an interview by letter.

What the Heck Is an Informational Interview?

If the word "interview" makes you quiver, relax. The type of interview I'm talking about in this chapter isn't the same as a job interview. Far from it.

Q & A

How can I lighten up my request for an informational interview?

If it feels appropriate, you might offer to take your interviewee to lunch or to bring box lunches or coffee to her office. In other words, make it both professional and enjoyable for your advisor so she'll look forward to your meeting and feel that you value her time. Even if she turns down your offer for a snack, she'll appreciate your thoughtfulness.

In an informational interview, you're not asking for a job, so you have nothing to lose. Your meeting is strictly for gathering information—that's why it's called an "informational" interview. In fact, the person you interview is not a hiring manager for the line of work you are investigating. Your interviewee is someone who *does* the type of work you are considering, so most likely she is not in a position to offer you a job.

For instance, if you are contemplating a career move into a customer service representative position and want to ask questions about what it's like to do that kind of work, you would have an *informational* interview with a customer service representative, not the manager of customer service. Later, if you apply for a customer service representative position, you would have a *job* interview with the manager of customer service.

Q & A

In an informational interview, who is the interviewer and who is the interviewee?

When you have an informational interview with a professional, you are the *interviewer* (because you're the one asking the questions) and the professional is the *interviewee* (the one being interviewed).

An Interview That Works

Informational interviewing is an extremely productive tool in conducting a job search. Here's what you can hope to gain from such an interview:

➤ You will gather the latest information in the industry and occupation you are looking into.

No matter how much research you have done about an industry or company, as you talk with your interviewee, you may hear news that hasn't yet reached (and may never reach) professional journals, newspapers, and on-line resources. For example, you might learn of an immediate crisis being faced by the company; a new product that hasn't hit the newsstands yet; or an expansion project that will lead to more employment opportunities than have been posted publicly.

➤ You will gain insight into what the job qualifications are, how realistic it is for you to pursue this new career, and how you might achieve that goal. For example:

Theresa thought that she might like to make a career change into furniture sales, so she arranged an informational interview with

Watch Out!
Be sure that nothing in your request for an interview threatens your reader. You don't want him to think that you're really after his job. Reassure him that you are not looking for a job—you simply want his advice before making your career decision.

CAUTION

Sarah, a furniture salesperson. When Sarah learned that Theresa had been an administrative assistant but had no sales experience, she recommended that Theresa apply to the furniture sales department as an administrative assistant and work her way up to a sales position from within the company. Sarah's advice, of course, was based on her insider's knowledge of hiring policies at her company.

➤ The professional you interview could become an important link in your job search network.

Once you have won the respect of your interviewee, you will have an ally in her field. Your new friend may be known in her profession, and having her as your advisor may lend credibility to you. With her permission, you might use her as a reference in your cover letter when applying for a job or drop her name during a job-hunt conversation.

➤ Your interviewee will undoubtedly have names of others who would be good for you to contact, either for more information or for applying for a job.

Never leave an informational interview without asking if your interviewee knows of anyone else who you could talk with. Almost everyone has a Rolodex or database of professional acquaintances and is willing to share connections with a sincere job seeker. So before you conclude your meeting, continue to build your job search network by asking, "Is there anyone else you suggest I contact?"

➤ Maybe, just maybe, you will learn of a job opening in your interviewee's company and you'll be able to apply for it on the spot.

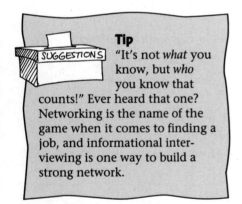

Tip

"It's not *what* you know, but *who* you know that counts!" Ever heard that one? Networking is the name of the game when it comes to finding a job, and informational interviewing is one way to build a strong network.

A job offer doesn't usually result from an informational interview, and you shouldn't go into your appointment with such an expectation, but it does happen from time to time. So be armed and ready with your resume, in case an employment opportunity arises—you just might get lucky!

Who on Earth Can Help Me?

Believe it or not, many professionals enjoy giving informational interviews. Like most of us, they're flattered to be asked for advice and are happy to help aspiring job seekers get started in something they themselves are excited about, namely their careers. How do you find someone to interview? Here are some possibilities:

1. Check with a career center to see if they have a list or database of professionals who have agreed to grant informational interviews.

2. Put the word out in your network of friends and associates that you're looking for someone to give you advice in your career move.

3. Use the Yellow Pages and resources at the business section of a library to identify companies in the industry you're considering. Then make cold calls to find the name of a professional who might be willing to spend some time answering career-related questions.

Learning the Ropes

I can't over stress how important it is to do research before requesting an informational interview. After all, the more you know about the new company, industry, market, etc. the more enticing your request can be and the more wisely you can use your precious 20 to 30 scheduled minutes to ask good questions. So take some time to create a company profile, which you learned about in Chapter 3, "Research Smarts."

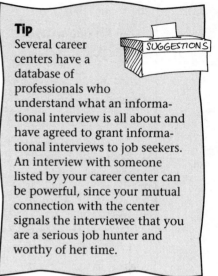

Tip
Several career centers have a database of professionals who understand what an informational interview is all about and have agreed to grant informational interviews to job seekers. An interview with someone listed by your career center can be powerful, since your mutual connection with the center signals the interviewee that you are a serious job hunter and worthy of her time.

A Few Questions, Please

Make a list of questions that you'd like to ask during your interview. For guidance in creating your list, glance through the following commonly asked questions. Your situation may require a unique set of questions to satisfy your curiosity about the career at hand, so think beyond this list to ensure the success of your interview.

COMMONLY ASKED QUESTIONS

1. What is a typical 9-to-5 day like for someone in your profession?
2. What are two or three major skills required for this job?
3. What kind of experience is usually expected of someone entering this field?
4. Would you share with me how you got into this line of work?
5. What part of your job do you love the most?
6. Could you comment on the industry culture with regard to (gender, age, disabilities, or some other issue)?
7. Generally speaking, what are the salary ranges for this profession—entry level to the ceiling?
8. Where do you see this industry heading in the next five years?
9. Is there anyone else you recommend I speak with to learn more about this profession?

continues

---

continued

Your list of questions

1. _____
   _____

2. _____
   _____

3. _____
   _____

4. _____
   _____

5. _____
   _____

6. _____
   _____

7. _____
   _____

8. _____
   _____

9. _____
   _____

10. _____
    _____

Q & A

How many questions should I prepare for my informational interview?

Since you expect only 20 or 30 minutes of a professional's time, ten good questions will be sufficient. There may not be time to ask them all, so prioritize them ahead of time to be sure you get your most important ones on the table.

A Written Invitation

Once you know who you want to ask for an informational interview, you need to ask him for a meeting.

Your letter should be brief—from two short paragraphs to three quarters of a page (not more than one page). Use the four-step, letter-writing process from Part 2 in the following way:

1. Observe the guidelines in Chapter 5, "Step One—Set the Stage," for constructing the heading, inside address, and salutation.

2. Create a lead paragraph (see Chapter 6, "Step Two—Follow My Lead") that establishes a personal connection with the reader. For instance:

   Your supervisor, Gail Simpson, has encouraged me to invite you to lunch.

   When I read your article in the Chronicle *last Sunday, I knew that I needed to meet you as soon as an opportunity arose.*

3. Design the middle paragraph as mentioned in Chapter 7, "Step Three—The Pitch," to tell the reader a little bit about yourself and a few points about your desire for a career change. For instance:

   I'm new to the Denver area and would appreciate an introduction to the city's resort industry. With five years of hospitality management under my belt, I'm interested to see how you think I could fit into the local business arena.

   Fortune 500 companies have always held an allure for me. I've "written" several of Gainsville's small business success stories, and now I think it's time to move to the big time.

4. Ask for an informational interview in a way that explains what an informational interview is (since many are not familiar with that term). For example:

   Would you have 20 minutes to talk to me about what it's like to do your line of work? I'm considering a career change, and would appreciate some insight into the field.

   I would be grateful if you had time for a brief meeting to offer me guidance on how I might get into your line of work.

In popping the question, here's the trick: Most people don't know what an informational interview is, at least not by that term. They do, however, understand words

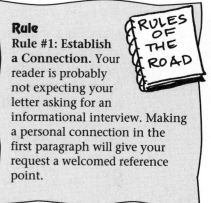

Rule

Rule #1: Establish a Connection. Your reader is probably not expecting your letter asking for an informational interview. Making a personal connection in the first paragraph will give your request a welcomed reference point.

Watch Out!

Don't be meek or apologetic when asking for an informational interview ("I hate to ask you this, but if it's not too much trouble, could you spare a minute ….") You're not begging for a handout or even asking for a job. Request an informational interview politely and confidently, thereby showing respect for both the interviewee and yourself.

like "advice," "suggestions," "guidance," "help," and "recommendations." So when you phrase your request, don't say, "May I have an informational interview with you?" That type of question will probably make the reader wrinkle up her face and say, "Informational interview? What is he talking about?" Instead, use lines like:

A discussion about your profession would help me figure out if computer programming is a good career move for me. Do you have 20 minutes sometime soon for us to meet?

5. Your closing statement is key since you want to leave the reader on a good note, and you want to initiate action: You'd like the professional to agree to an informational interview. Thank your reader for his time and, using a tactful approach, offer to call him to set something up. Your line of instigation should be polite and respectful. Try something like one of these:

For your convenience, I'll call you to see when you are free for coffee.

May we talk on the phone about possible times to meet? I'll call your office in a few days.

The next letter demonstrates how to write an effective request for an informational interview.

Larry Cook
001 Champion Court
Fremont, CA 92733
(123) 123-1234

February 16, 199X

Mr. Michael Cohen
Regional Sales Representative
Higher Formulations Pharmaceuticals, Inc.
01 Hedgewood Drive
Fremont, CA 92730

By mentioning the name of the reader's friend, Larry paves the way for his request.

Dear Mr. Cohen,

At a luncheon last week, Jim Spolan gave me your card with the recommendation, "Larry, you really should talk to Michael Cohen. He's the best in the business."

This may come as a surprise to you, but I'm not looking for a job — not yet, anyway. I'm considering a career move from high-tech sales to pharmaceutical sales; but before making that jump, I'd like to learn more about your industry.

May I take you out to lunch and engage you in such a conversation?

After all Mike has told me about your history at Higher Formulations, I'm sure I have a lot to learn from you. Next week, I'll give you a call in hopes that you can squeeze some time into your calendar for me. Thank you.

Sincerely,

Without using the term "informational interview," Larry asks for a meeting.

Larry Cook

Good Follow-Up Builds Bridges

After your informational interview, be sure to follow up with a thank-you letter. Your interviewee's generosity deserves gratitude, whether or not the interview turned out the way you thought it would. Remember, she is now a part of your network and you can strengthen your connection with her by expressing your thanks.

To learn how to write a thank-you letter for an informational interview, turn to Chapter 14, "Thank You Very Much."

The Least You Need to Know

➤ An informational interview is a 20 to 30 minute meeting with someone who works at a job that you are considering for your next career move.

➤ Find someone for an informational interview by asking those in your personal and professional network, inquiring at career centers, and making cold calls to companies of interest.

➤ Research the company and person you will be interviewing and create a list of questions to ask.

➤ A request for an interview can be made in person, by phone, or by letter. If asking in writing, follow the four-step letter writing process, ending with a polite query for a meeting.

➤ Always send a thank-you note after your informational interview.

Chapter 14

Thank You Very Much

In This Chapter

➤ How to enhance your chances for the job by sending a dynamite thank-you letter

➤ Learn to put your best foot forward with a thank-you note for your job acceptance

➤ Find out why thanking an employer after he has rejected you may keep you in the running for a job

➤ How to show appreciation for an informational interview

➤ Thanking the members of your network for their help

Always say "thank you"—a tried and true notion that works wonders. It's amazing what a simple "thank you" can do to brighten your coworker's day, raise a friend's self-esteem, or... influence a prospective employer to hire you.

A word of thanks could be appropriate before, during, and after your job search, including (gulp!) if you get a job rejection. This chapter looks at five types of thank-you letters you may need to write during your job hunt.

Q & A

In an employer's eyes, will I seem like a pest if I send a thank-you letter?

You can say "thank you" without being a pest. A short note is a great way to show gratitude without taking much of an employer's time.

A Round of Applause for the Job Interview

After a job interview, a letter of sincere thanks is much appreciated by an employer. He took a chunk out of his busy day to give you the opportunity to win a job, so this is the time for you to say "thanks" in writing and to use your thank-you letter as an opportunity to build your relationship with him.

Here are two scenarios to demonstrate the benefits of a thank-you note.

Here's to a Good Meeting

You've just returned from an interview and you feel pretty good about how it went. In fact, you liked the hiring manager and his company so much, you want the job even more than before the interview. So what can you do to increase your chances of getting the position? How about sending a thank-you letter that underscores your qualifications?

The Not-So-Good Interview

You've completed a so-so job interview and as you walk away from it, you realize that you were nervous and didn't perform as well as you could have. You really want this job—you like the job description and the company atmosphere is a good match for your working style. But how can you reverse the bad impression you may have made at your interview? How about writing a confident thank-you note that emphasizes once more your strong qualifications?

The Nitty Gritty

A thank-you letter can run from two short paragraphs to three quarters of a page—definitely not more than one page. Let's look at how the letter-writing process from Part 2, "Your Resume Booster," applies to your thank-you letter.

1. Follow the guidelines in Chapter 5, "Step One—Set the Stage," for constructing the heading, inside address, and salutation.

2. Create a catchy lead paragraph (see Chapter 6, "Step Two—Follow My Lead") that offers appreciation for your job interview. For example:

*Even in my short career, I've been on several job
interviews. My meeting with you last Tuesday was
by far the most informative and inspiring.*

*Yesterday's interview was well worth my flight to
and from New York!*

3. Design the middle paragraph as mentioned in
   Chapter 7, "Step Three—The Pitch," to reinforce
   the strengths you talked about in your interview, or to promote ones that you haven't yet
   brought up. Just as in a cover letter, you can
   present your qualifications, using bullets points
   (•) or short paragraphs. For example:

*After hearing how you built Tower's marketing
department from scratch, I realize that what I have
to offer as your assistant is:*

- *An adept ear for instructions and strong organizational skills to implement them.*
- *The ability to keep things running smoothly without drawing attention to the details of the operation.*
- *A talent to motivate my crew, while nurturing morale.*

*Shortly after I got onto the plane, I came up with a plan of attack for the sandstone
research project we discussed. My strategy involves fewer scientists and a tighter deadline.*

4. Thank the employer once more and initiate the next move (in this case, probably
   the next interview or an announcement of applicant acceptance), keeping the ball
   in your court, if possible. For example:

*You mentioned that you would be making your choice for the assistant position next
Wednesday. Since I will be traveling on business that week, I will call you from the road to
learn of your decision.*

*Realizing that you have many things on your mind at this time of year, I will call your
assistant in a week to hear the results of your selection process.*

Notice how the next thank-you letter applies the four letter-writing steps.

> **Rule**
> **Rule #2: Show
> Personality.** Now
> that you've met the
> hiring manager in
> the job interview, you
> have a sense of his personality.
> Since you've started developing
> a rapport with him, you can let
> your hair down a little (staying
> on the professional side, of
> course) in your thank-you note.

RULES OF THE ROAD

Bill Daly
0010 Church Street, Apt. 4
San Francisco, CA 94114
123/123-1234

August 13, 199X

Bill's lead paragraph expresses appreciation for his interview.

Ms. Margaret Hillman
Executive Program Manager
Federal Union Bank
001 Downer Street
Redwood City, CA 94305

Bill reinforces his qualifications in paragraph # 2.

Dear Ms. Hillman,

Thank you for spending such quality time with me yesterday. I especially enjoyed hearing about your business goals for the next five years, and found myself sharing your vision of 32 new branches in California by 1999.

One point I forgot to mention when we spoke: I worked closely with my current supervisor to develop the training program now used in all new Eureka Savings offices nationwide.

I appreciate your giving me your direct phone number. I'll call you in two weeks, as you suggested, once your applicant review is completed.

Again, thank you!

Very truly yours,

The ball stays in Bill's court when he closes his letter.

Bill Daly

Muchas Gracias for Giving Me the Job!

Congratulations! Between your professional qualifications and your magical charm, you got the job!

Before you pack your briefcase for your first day at work, I suggest you take a moment to write a brief thank-you note to your new boss. Here's why:

Rule

Rule #4: Make It Quick and Easy to Read. Your thank-you-for-the-job letter should be very brief and centered on its page, with lots of white space incorporated into its layout.

➤ You're genuinely grateful he awarded you the job.

➤ The employer knows that his decision to hire you is a test of his judgment. A thank-you letter is one way to reassure him that he made the right choice to bring you on board.

A two-paragraph note will do the trick. Here are guidelines for constructing your note:

1. Use Chapter 5, to get help with the heading, inside address, and salutation.

2. Start with a lead paragraph (see Chapter 6, that offers gratitude for your acceptance, using a personality that reflects the rapport developed during your interview. For example:

   I'm very excited about starting my adventure at Blacksmiths. Thank you!

   Thank you for your vote of confidence! I look forward to joining your team.

3. Write a quick wrap-up that says you'll be there for work on the appointed day. For example:

   I'll see you Monday, March 3rd, for the beginning of our creative venture together.

   Next Monday, I'll be in your office, ready for my first dynamic day at Long's Drugs.

To see a thank-you note for job acceptance, take a peek at the following one by Bob Kidd.

BOB KIDD
01 Nexess Lane
Powers Point, MO 53923
(123) 123-1234

June 23, 199X

Mr. Leo Somplex
Producer
World Wide Ventures
011 Windsor Ave.
Colgate, MO 53920

> A quick "thank you" that took only minutes to write helps set the tone that will last for years on Bob's new job.

Dear Mr. Somplex:

What a pleasure to hear that I won the job as your traveling photographer. Thank you!

I see my new position as an opportunity to further the company's mission statement, starting bright and early Monday, July 7th.

Again, thanks very much for giving me this opportunity to work with you.

Yours,

> This very short note is sincere and energetic.

Bob Kidd

Thanks a Lot for the Rejection

Ouch! You didn't get the job!

Getting a rejection announcement for a job you really want is a tough "no" to hear. Despite knowing that your job hunt is bound to have its disappointments, it's hard to face a negative response when you put so much time and energy into your job application.

Even though you may feel down and out over a particular job rejection, take a moment to realize the employer's position. Making a hiring decision isn't always easy. She may have had a devil of a time choosing between you and a few others of equal standing. Maybe the race was really close and you were a near winner.

It's Not Over 'til...

After all the work you put into this job request, don't you think it's worth one more attempt at landing the job or at least using your connection with your interviewer to network for another job? Use the following steps to write a thank-you note to your interviewer:

1. According to Chapter 5 create your heading, inside address, and salutation.

2. In your lead paragraph (see Chapter 6, express gratitude for the time and consideration your interviewer invested in you, along with regret at not having received the job. For example:

   I appreciated the valuable insight you shared with me during my interview for accountant. When your assistant told me that I was not selected for the position, I was disappointed—but not discouraged.

> **Rule**
> **Rule #2: Show Personality.** A "thank you" after getting turned down for a job demonstrates good character. It shows that you don't have a chip on your shoulder for having lost the contest.

3. In the mid-section of your note, state your continued interest in the job. Should the position become vacant, you'd like another shot at it. Who knows, the chosen candidate may not accept the job or he might not work out in the company. For example:

   Please keep me in mind if the position reopens unexpectedly.

   Knowing that you are restructuring your organization, I will keep my eyes open for other opportunities at Saunders.

4. Wrap up your letter with a request for a referral for a similar job in the same company. In making your query, keep the ball in your court by saying that you will call the reader for the answer. For example:

Tip

If you didn't win the job you were after, a thank-you letter may be just the ticket for keeping your foot in the door with the hiring manager. Who knows, maybe an even *better* job will arise and you'll be invited to fill it.

Is there someone else at Towels Unlimited or within the industry who you recommend I speak with about job opportunities? I will contact you at the end of the week to see if you have a few telephone numbers for me.

You mentioned that your division in Los Angeles is expanding. May I call your office next week to get the manager's name and number?

The following thank-you letter was written in response to a job rejection.

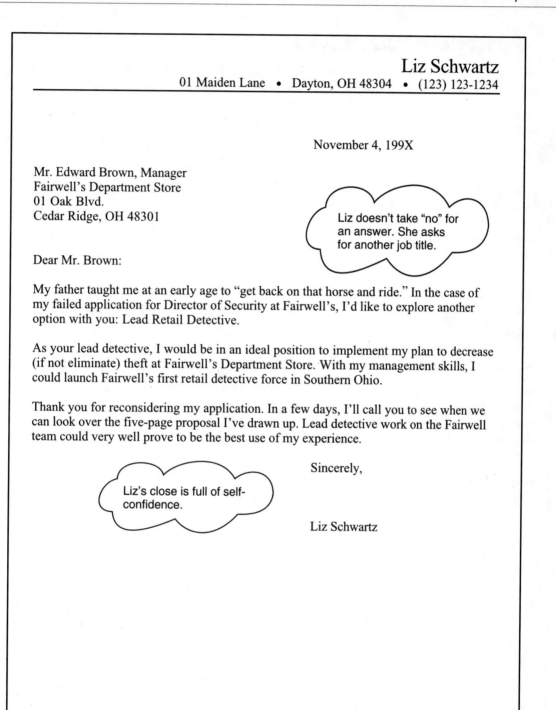

Liz Schwartz

01 Maiden Lane • Dayton, OH 48304 • (123) 123-1234

November 4, 199X

Mr. Edward Brown, Manager
Fairwell's Department Store
01 Oak Blvd.
Cedar Ridge, OH 48301

Liz doesn't take "no" for an answer. She asks for another job title.

Dear Mr. Brown:

My father taught me at an early age to "get back on that horse and ride." In the case of my failed application for Director of Security at Fairwell's, I'd like to explore another option with you: Lead Retail Detective.

As your lead detective, I would be in an ideal position to implement my plan to decrease (if not eliminate) theft at Fairwell's Department Store. With my management skills, I could launch Fairwell's first retail detective force in Southern Ohio.

Thank you for reconsidering my application. In a few days, I'll call you to see when we can look over the five-page proposal I've drawn up. Lead detective work on the Fairwell team could very well prove to be the best use of my experience.

Liz's close is full of self-confidence.

Sincerely,

Liz Schwartz

I Appreciate Your Advice

A thank-you letter for an informational interview (you learned about that type of interview in Chapter 13, "Sending an SOS") is like sending a thank-you note for a present. After all, your interviewee gave you a gift of her time and information.

Tip

Having your informational interviewee in your corner of the ring may prove valuable in your job hunt. A polite thank-you note will foster a lasting relationship.

Tip

Your informational interviewee probably has many people in her professional life. When you write your thank-you letter, you may need to slip in a reminder about how she knows you. For instance, you could reference the day, place, or memorable aspect of your meeting together.

Watch Out!

Since your interviewee has already been generous with her time, be careful not to wear out your welcome by asking for too much. If you need to make a request, help your reader out by doing as much of the work as possible (for instance, if you ask her to mail you information, enclose a self-addressed, stamped envelope).

Your letter of thanks should be sincere and brief. Here are some guidelines:

1. Generate your letterhead and then input the inside address and salutation for your informational interviewee. (See Chapter 5)

2. Write a lead paragraph (see Chapter 6) that expresses gratitude for your recent meeting with your reader. For example:

   Our conversation last Wednesday was just "what the doctor ordered" for me. Thank you!

   Your career advice to me was right on the button, Mr. Boyles. I appreciated every word of it!

3. In your second paragraph, share a brief update on your job search or thank her for something special from the meeting (perhaps she gave you a valuable lead or piece of advice). For example:

   As soon as I got home, I hopped onto my computer and requested the list of doctors from the California Ophthalmology Association, as you suggested.

   I already have a hot lead, after following your suggestion to call the home owners' association in my town.

4. In the final paragraph of your letter, thank your interviewee once more. Initiate action *only* if it's appropriate. For example:

   You mentioned that you wanted to send me a list of companies in Illinois. I have enclosed a self-addressed, stamped envelop for your convenience.

   May I call upon you if I need more advice down the road?

The next thank-you letter shows appreciation for an informational interview.

PEGGY HENDERSON
0010 Outback Road
Louisville, OR 96022
(123) 123-1234

April 16, 199X

Sandra Hayes
Project Manager
Northwestern Lumber Association
0012 Southern Blvd.
Louisville, OR 96021

> A sincere note of gratitude begins Peggy's letter.

Dear Sandra,

During our meeting last Wednesday, I learned more about the lumber industry than from all my other research thus far. Thank you very much for sharing your information and your contacts at Franklin Logging.

I called Mr. Franklin, and he agreed to meet with me in early May. It promises to be a fruitful discussion.

Again, thank you for your advice.

Sincerely,

> Peggy shows good follow-through in her second paragraph.

Peggy Henderson

The Good News Letter

Now that you've landed a job, don't forget your pals who helped you along the way. It's time to give special thanks to the members of your network who brainstormed with you over coffee, allowed you to use them as references, gave you names and phone numbers of valued contacts, and lent their moral support every step of your job search journey.

Certainly calling them up or seeing them in person is a gracious way of saying "thank you." Another way is to write a "good news letter." A good news letter is a letter or card that announces the success of your job search and shows appreciation for your friends' support.

Here's how to produce your good news letter:

1. Develop your letterhead, referring to Chapter 5, if you need assistance. Notice on the next page that a good news letter does not need an inside address or salutation since it is clearly an announcement being sent to several people.

2. Write a punchy, one- or two-sentence paragraph that announces your new job. Since you're friendly with the members of your network (they're your friends, relatives, and colleagues), it's OK to use a familiar, joyous tone. Example:

   Finally… the job of my dreams. I got the position writing jokes for sitcoms at Blissville. (Yep, that's really my employer's name!)

   Here's a hand to my friends who helped me get my new job. I'm now a sales rep for Cellular One. (Yeah, a round of free phone calls on me!)

3. Thank your buddies for their help. Example:

   Seriously, I owe you all many thanks for your support.

   Thank you all for being so generous with your advice over the last two months.

4. This announcement is informal, so there's no need for a complimentary close or printed name. Just sign your announcement by hand.

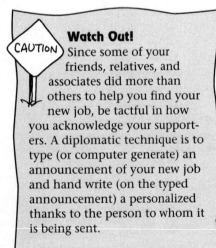

Watch Out! Since some of your friends, relatives, and associates did more than others to help you find your new job, be tactful in how you acknowledge your supporters. A diplomatic technique is to type (or computer generate) an announcement of your new job and hand write (on the typed announcement) a personalized thanks to the person to whom it is being sent.

Here's a sample of a good news letter by Clark Talbott.

CLARK TALBOTT

0011 Westchester Drive ✪ San Francisco, CA 94115
(123) 123-1234

April 16, 199X

This fun letter spreads Clark's good news and thanks to his friends and associates.

Good news! Not only did I get my patriotic donation to the IRS in on time — I also landed a new job! I'm now the proud Sales Support Supervisor at Rondel's Round the Clock (at 4th and Brandon).

Thanks for your good thoughts and generous efforts. You really helped make my job hunt successful!

Sam,

Special thanks for turning me on to Philip Halstead. He was my hot ticket to the hiring manager. I owe you!

Clark

A handwritten addendum personalizes each letter Clark sends out.

The Least You Need to Know

➤ You should send a thank-you letter to your interviewer after the meeting. Your letter should indicate gratitude and a sincere desire for the job you're after.

➤ When you get accepted for a job, send a thank-you letter to the hiring manager to demonstrate your enthusiasm for joining his team and to assure him that he made the right choice in hiring you.

➤ Even if you didn't win the job you were after, a thank-you note to the employer may keep you in the lineup for the job or another job like it.

➤ Always write a thank-you letter to someone who has granted you an informational interview.

➤ Write a note to members of your network, announcing your new job and thanking those who helped you on your job hunt.

Part 5
The ABCs of Good Writing Technique

Ever wonder who wrote the English language? I mean, who the heck made up all the words, figured out how to string them together to form sentences, and then sprinkled in punctuation marks?

Of course, no one person created our glorious language—it's the product of centuries of use and change by people like you and me. And it's still evolving as we speak! That's right, you and I have a say in its growth as we coin words, question the logic of punctuation, and even rebel against grammar rules (such as the use of gender-specific pronouns like "he" and "she").

Part 5 presents some grammar rules as they stand today and tips on how to construct sentences that deliver a friendly, confident attitude. It also discusses techniques for breaking writer's block so that you can get your masterful sentences on paper and in the mail to your next employer.

Good Technique Helps

In This Chapter

➤ Understanding how punctuation facilitates meaning

➤ Know what and when words should be capitalized

➤ How to juggle apostrophes and S's to make nouns plural and possessive

Why do most of us freeze when we hear the word *grammar*? We express ourselves out loud, usually without thinking about our sentence structure or where to insert commas and periods. But as soon as we get our pen (or keyboards) in hand, putting together sentences seems like a monumental task.

If you suffer from "grammarphobia," relax. It doesn't have to be a daunting task to write a good letter, especially since I'm going to help you out.

This chapter presents a brief overview of grammar concepts (otherwise known as *rules*) to help you pen a grammatically correct letter. For a comprehensive look at grammar, refer to a handbook such as *The Complete Idiot's Guide to Grammar and Style*.

The Point of Punctuation

Punctuation is every writer's buddy. Without punctuation, sentences would ramble on until they fell off the page, phrases would lose their relevance, and statements would have as much expression as a faceless mannequin. By adding a period here, a comma there, and an exclamation mark once in a while, your composition comes to life.

The Meaning Behind It All

To ensure that your cover letter has meaning, you need to slip your punctuation buddies in between some of your words. With just a few guidelines, you'll be armed and ready to punctuate your letter like a pro.

Let's go over the eight types of punctuation you're apt to use in your letter. Here they are:

➤ Period (.)

➤ Question mark (?)

➤ Exclamation mark (!)

➤ Comma (,)

➤ Semicolon (;)

➤ Colon (:)

➤ Quotation marks (")

➤ Apostrophe (')

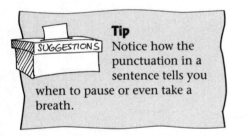

Tip
Notice how the punctuation in a sentence tells you when to pause or even take a breath.

To make sure that you put the right marks in the right places, here's a brief overview.

1. Periods

➤ Place a period at the end of a statement or command:

Mr. Jones recommended that I send you my resume.

➤ A period is optional at the end of each phrase in a list:

Over the last ten years, I have developed an expertise in:

- *Juggling multiple tasks at once.*
- *Delegating tasks appropriately.*
- *Providing detailed analyses promptly.*

or

> *Over the last ten years, I have developed an expertise in:*
> - *Juggling multiple tasks at once*
> - *Delegating tasks appropriately*
> - *Providing detailed analyses promptly*

➤ A period should appear after abbreviations:

> *I use the P.A.R. (Problem, Action, Result) approach when dealing with issues.*
>
> *Inc.* (incorporated)

An exception to this rule is with academic degrees, in which case the periods are optional:

M.B.A. or MBA

> **Watch Out!** CAUTION
> The use of question and exclamation marks is sometimes just the ticket for nabbing a reader's attention. However, these expressive marks should not be overused.

2. Question Marks

➤ Put a question mark at the end of a direct question:

Will you be in your office next week?

➤ A question mark may be positioned after each of several consecutive words or phrases that are questions in response to a longer question immediately before the series:

Did you ever wonder how Lucite got most of our market share? Was it skill? Timing? Or just plain luck?

3. Exclamation Marks

➤ Exclamation marks should appear at the end of statements of strong feeling such as surprise, enthusiasm, pride, and so on:

What a winner!

➤ An exclamation mark may replace a question mark if the question is also an exclamation:

How could I resist!

➤ An exclamation mark is sometimes placed inside parentheses immediately after a word in a sentence in order to give that word punch:

If I have to crawl (!) across George's office, I'll get General Motors to agree.

➤ Place an exclamation mark after an expressive word that precedes a related sentence:

Oh! Did I tell you the results of the race?

Q & A

What's the difference between a phrase and a clause?

A phrase is a group of words that does not have a subject and a verb and when standing alone is not a complete sentence. A clause is a group of words that has a subject and verb. It can grammatically stand on its own as a complete sentence.

4. Commas

➤ Within a sentence, commas may be used to set off words, phrases, and clauses that are not essential to the sentence:

I drew up a sales plan, primarily for the West Coast, that requires new contracts in Los Angeles.

Your plan, therefore, is without regard to the East Coast sales representatives.

In the revision of your plan, although you shouldn't attempt to rewrite it too soon, please make sure to include the East Coast.

➤ Place a comma just before words, phrases, and clauses that serve as an afterthought at the end of the sentence:

I spoke before the board of directors, in the capacity of advisor and friend.

➤ Commas should separate elements of a date. However, no comma is needed when just the month and year are stated:

Wednesday, June 24, 1997   *June 1997*

➤ Insert a comma between a person's name and an abbreviation that follows his name, except when the abbreviation is "Jr." or "Sr."

John Meirs, M.D.   *John Meirs Jr.*

➤ Use a comma to separate two or more parts of a compound sentence. If the parts are long or complex, a semicolon (instead of a comma) is used between the clauses:

I am very happy to accommodate your schedule, especially since I will be in your area on that day anyway.

I am very happy to accommodate your schedule; especially since I have a dentist appointment, shopping, and other errands in your area on that day.

➤ Commas are placed between three or more items in a series:

I bring skills, experience, and perseverance to the bargaining table.

Also correct:

I bring skills, experience and perseverance to the bargaining table.

➤ Position a comma between two or more adjectives:

Your company holds the oldest, qualified speakers in the business.

➤ No comma is necessary before Inc. or Ltd. in the name of a company, unless the firm elects to have a comma there:

Century Home Realty Inc.

➤ If an address is written as part of a sentence, the commas are placed between each element of the address, except between the state and zip code:

927 Homestead Lane, Fort Worth, Texas 62938

➤ Insert commas in a sentence to clarify meaning, if necessary:

As you know, everything went as planned.

➤ Place a comma after the salutation in a letter. If the letter is of a formal business nature, a colon may be used instead of a comma in the salutation.

Dear Mr. Peterson,
Dear Mr. Peterson:

> **Watch Out!**
> The comma is one of the most overused punctuation marks. Here's a technique for avoiding unnecessary use of commas in your writing. First take all commas out of your sentence. Then put each comma back into the sentence *only* if eliminating the comma would break a specific grammar rule or would make the meaning of the sentence unclear.

5. Semicolons

➤ A semicolon should be placed between two independent clauses:

Matilda's Hotsprings isn't always the first to open every spring; sometimes it's open year-round.

Tip
Instead of having two consecutive short sentences, see if a semicolon could combine the shorties into one comprehensive sentence.

➤ Semicolons are used between phrases in a series if the phrases are long or if any of the phrases have commas within them:

When deciding among candidates, please remember I'm the one who recently broke all production records in Mississippi; brought the competition to it's knees in the display contest; and got Steely's Safety Pins featured in the press.

6. Colons

➤ Insert a colon at the end of a statement to introduce a related list of words, phrases, or clauses:

I don't like to brag, but I have to tell you that I have:

tenacity

street sense

bargaining power

➤ A colon may be used after a phrase that introduces a clause:

For instance: I've always met sales quotas in all my positions.

7. Quotation Marks

➤ Quotation marks begin and end a statement to indicate that the words are the exact words spoken by someone.

The president exclaimed, "This is the year of expansion!"

➤ Quotation marks may be used around a word or phrase that is an object being spoken about in the sentence.

He has coined the phrase "hygienic transference."

➤ Place quotation marks around words and phrases used ironically, humorously, or to mean something other than what they usually mean.

I applied to the hospital for a "Band-Aid" job.

8. Apostrophes

> **Tip**
> Do not use an apostrophe to indicate the plural form of a number. For instance: *It happened back in the 1980s.*

➤ Place an apostrophe followed by an "s" after common and proper nouns to indicate possession. If the noun is plural, put the apostrophe after the "s":

Singular possessive: This is Frank's desk. It is made from South America's finest wood. The desk's finish is clear and shiny.

Plural possessive: The officials checked North and South Americas' customs departments to ensure compliance. All the sales representatives' quotas have been raised.

➤ Use an apostrophe to replace a missing number in a date:

He graduated in the class of '76.

➤ An apostrophe is inserted in a contraction in place of one or more missing letters:

don't, can't

➤ An apostrophe may be used as a single quotation mark before and after a word, phrase, or sentence that would normally be surrounded by quotation marks, except that it is part of the text that appears within quotation marks:

Michael said, "I started the interview by saying, 'Of all the places I've considered, this is the company I'd love to work for.' Everything went smoothly from then on."

Capitalizing on Letters

Here's a topic that throws a lot of letter writers for a loop: capitalization. Knowing what words always start with a capital letter and what circumstances require a normally lowercase word to be capitalized can make a big difference in how effectively you communicate. Keep the following points in mind about capitalization as you plow through your letter-writing process:

> **Watch Out!**
> Do not capitalize the word "the" when it appears before the name of an organization, unless "the" is officially part of the organization's name. (Examples: *I wrote to the Agency on Aging. I wrote to The American Red Cross Association.*)

➤ Capitalize the first word of a sentence, question, exclamation, or expression used as a sentence.

➤ Capitalize the first word of a quoted sentence, even when it appears within a sentence:

I couldn't believe it when Mr. Jones said, "Go for it!"

➤ Capitalize the first word of each line in a list of items.

➤ The first word of the salutation and complimentary close should be capitalized.

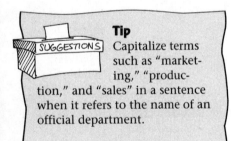

Q & A

Should I capitalize a job title in the text of my cover letter?

Capitalizing a job title is optional. You may capitalize the title if you want to give it emphasis. If you capitalize one job title in your letter, you should capitalize all job titles in that document.

Tip

SUGGESTIONS Capitalize terms such as "marketing," "production," and "sales" in a sentence when it refers to the name of an official department.

Watch Out!

CAUTION As a rule, do not capitalize a professional title when it is used as a common noun. (Example: *Please ask the president your question.*) Capitalize a title when it is used as part of someone's name. (Example: *Please ask President Brown your question.*)

➤ Capitalize proper nouns such as names of people, organizations, days of the week, months, and languages:

Sally White, Produce Growers Inc., Monday, March, English

➤ Capitalize adjectives that are derived from proper nouns:

South American bananas

➤ Capitalize common nouns when incorporated into a proper name:

President Higgins, Professor Anders

➤ Capitalize the first and last word in a title, as well as all words within the title that are four or more letters long or have special significance:

The Annual Tin and Aluminum Report

Getting Possessive

Now let's get a feel for how to make nouns possessive. Here are four guidelines that are apt to come in handy while writing your letter.

➤ To make the possessive form of a singular noun that does not end in an "s" sound, add "'s":

man's salary　　　*Nevada's deserts*

➤ To create the possessive form of a noun that ends in the "s" sound, use the following guidelines: If the possessive form creates a new syllable, add "'s" at the end of the word. If an added syllable is awkward, simply add an apostrophe at the end of the word:

boss's decision, Dallas's mayor, Los Angeles' freeways, Mrs. Phillips' file

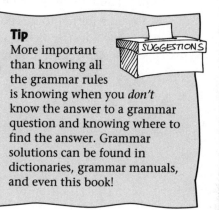

Tip
More important than knowing all the grammar rules is knowing when you *don't* know the answer to a grammar question and knowing where to find the answer. Grammar solutions can be found in dictionaries, grammar manuals, and even this book!

➤ To make the possessive form of a plural noun that ends in "s" or "es," add only an apostrophe at the end of the word:

investors' stock　　　*agencies' workforce*

➤ To create the possessive form of a plural noun that does not end in "s" or "es," add "'s":

women's wear　　　*children's toys*

Resources That Can Save Your Life... or at Least Your Career

With this chapter open while you write your job search correspondence, you've got a handy reference for technical questions that might come up. You might also want to keep some other resources handy. Ones that I like to have within an arm's reach of my desk are:

➤ A dictionary
➤ A thesaurus
➤ A writer's manual for grammar and style:
    The Complete Idiot's Guide to Grammar and Style
    The Gregg Reference Manual by William A. Sabin
    Elements of Style by Strunk and White
    Manual for Writers by Kate Turabian

In addition to these books, you can rely on some computer-friendly tools. Your word processing program probably has a spellchecker and thesaurus, which can offer solutions to writing problems in a few seconds. There's nothing like pulling out all your guns to write a smashing letter!

The Least You Need to Know

➤ Punctuation is used to clarify meaning and add expression to sentences.

➤ Capitalize proper nouns, titles of books, the pronoun "I," and words when they begin sentences.

➤ To make most singular nouns possessive, add "'s." Most plural nouns are made plural by simply adding an apostrophe at the end of the word.

➤ In addition to this book, other useful resources for learning writing technique include: the dictionary, a thesaurus, a grammar book, and aides such as the spellchecker found on your computer.

Chapter 16

Style Is Everything

In This Chapter

➤ Why exaggerated formality in your letter might turn off an employer

➤ Techniques for demonstrating confidence and sincerity through your writing

➤ Putting together sentences—even complicated ones

➤ Using verbs to demonstrate dynamism

➤ A list of frequently confused and misused words

It's not only *what* you say—it's also *how* you say it that counts. Aside from the content of your letter, the tone of your writing can influence an employer's hiring decision.

This chapter explains how to word your sentences to convey a winning attitude. It also covers some commonly made errors in sentence composition.

You Gotta Love My Personality

I've been chanting the word "personality" all through this book. Now we're going to examine exactly how to inject personality into your sentences. Yes, there are techniques for doing that—and you can easily learn them!

Stilted Language Spells Boredom

Right off the bat, I want to warn you about the biggest mistake made by most cover letter writers: They try to sound *dreadfully* professional—to the point of seeming artificial. Stilted language just doesn't cut it when you're trying to develop a relationship with your prospective employer. Here are some examples of what I mean by stilted language:

Enclosed, please find my resume for... (Reads like it's from a stuffed shirt!)

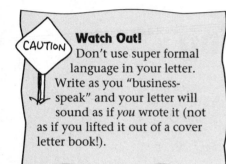

CAUTION

Watch Out!
Don't use super formal language in your letter. Write as you "business-speak" and your letter will sound as if *you* wrote it (not as if you lifted it out of a cover letter book!).

Pursuant of our conversation, I would like to apply for... (Sounds like a legal document, not a rapport-builder!)

In response to your advertisement in the Gazette, *I am enclosing...* (Too stiff!)

Get the picture? The types of statements above sound overly formal and go totally against the second Rule of the Road: Show Personality. The purpose of your cover letter is to grab the reader's attention and hold it. If your letter makes you sound stiff as a board, your reader will quickly get b-o-r-e-d.

Writing Between the Lines

Most people are more than a little intimidated by the art of writing. As a result, they tend to be extra formal in an effort to phrase things "just so." I'll bet you've received a letter that cries out, "Whoever wrote this is rigid!" But when you actually met the author of the stodgy document, you found her to be quite personable. "If only she had shown a little of her cheerful spirit in her memo," you thought. "I would have wanted to meet her sooner."

So as not to make the same mistake as the poor letter writer mentioned above, discover alternatives to formal language in your letter. Here are three suggestions:

➤ Do the exercises in Chapter 17, "Breaking Through Writer's Block," to loosen up your creative writing muscles.

➤ Refer to Part 2, "Your Resume Booster," where you'll find lists of dynamite phrases.

➤ Get inspiration from the sample letters throughout this book.

➤ Read ahead to discover some specific wording techniques for exuding your personality.

Be Yourself

You're really a terrific person and you should let your employer see that from the personality revealed in your letter. Let it all hang out—well, at least the good stuff.

Remember the personality list you compiled way back in Chapter 3, "Research Smarts"? It's time to pull it out and look at the traits you checked off as ones you want your prospective employer to know about. That's the "real" you that you want to pour into your writing.

In addition to the ones on your list, here are two characteristics that are always valued by bosses: confidence and sincerity. Let's explore how to infuse your sentences with these two champion qualities.

Confidence—The Winning Ticket

Your letter is your chance to be confident in black and white. When given a choice between wording that's "iffy" and wording that's confident, pick the latter. After all, if *you* don't sound like you believe in yourself, you can't very well expect a prospective employer—someone who's probably never met you—to believe in you. Your cover letter is a preview of who you are and how you approach challenges (you know, those times when confidence really comes into play!).

Whether you're making your initial introduction with a lead sentence, delivering your sales pitch in your middle paragraph, or initiating action at the end of your letter, use words and phrases that convey confidence.

The following examples contrast insecure and confident approaches.

> **Tip**
> Reading your letter out loud to yourself will help you catch stilted words and phrases. When you're happy with your letter, read it to a friend and ask: "Does this sound like me?"

> **Watch Out!**
> Don't start too many sentences (especially the ones that begin paragraphs) with the word "I." It's OK to use "I" to start a few sentences, but don't overdo it. You don't want the reader to look at your letter and say "I, I, I! Can't this guy think of anyone except himself?"

Insecure	Confident
I'll call you next week to see *if* we can meet.	I'll call you next week to see *when* we can meet.
I hope that I meet your qualifications for the job.	*I am confident* that I can do the job.
I might be a good candidate for the job.	*I am* the candidate for the job.
Hopefully we can get together to talk.	*Let's* get together to talk.
Perhaps I might meet with you.	*I'd like to* meet with you.
Maybe sometime next week we could find time to meet.	*Next week is* a good time for me to meet with you.
I was wondering if you have any job openings in sales.	*I'm inquiring about* availability in your sales department.

221

Sincerity Shines Through

Above all, be sincere in everything you say and the way you say it. Your reader will sense your earnestness and be impressed.

After doing your employer research (Chapter 3), you know why you truly want to work for the employer and how you fit into his organization. That's the sincere message you have to deliver. Your sincerity will signal the reader that you're a serious job candidate and you deserve his attention.

Here are some ways to deliver your heartfelt message:

➤ Use concrete terminology when you make claims about your qualifications. For instance, instead of using the vague phrase "responsible for," use an action verb such as "managed" so that the reader will know exactly what your role was. Also, use numbers (figures that indicate money, percentages, amount of circulation, etc.) to quantify your results, making the experience more believable.

Rule

Rule #2: Show Personality. The personality shown in your cover letter can help a prospective employer figure out whether or not you'd fit into his company culture. Sure, it's risky to show your true personality, but would you really want a job where you had to *pretend* to be someone other than yourself? Of course not! So, in your letter, why pretend to be someone you're not?

➤ Demonstrate that you understand the employer's business and know what you're getting into. Do this by speaking in terms peculiar to the company's goals, challenges, market, etc., as you learned about in Chapter 7, "Step Three—The Pitch."

➤ Insert your reader's name into the text of your letter to assure him that you really are talking specifically to *him*. (For an example of this technique, turn to Ron Landstrom's letter in the Appendix.)

➤ If your letter has a light, casual air, break that tone at one point with a phrase such as:

Seriously, I can do…

Joking aside, I can do…

I'm sincere when I say…

➤ Show that you truly want a job at the employer's firm, and that you're willing to do everything you can to get a stab at it. In your closing paragraph, tell the reader that you will call him (if you have his phone number) or take whatever step is appropriate toward nailing down an interview. (See Chapter 8, "Step Four—Closing the Sale," for tips on effective closing lines.)

➤ Offer a polite, simple, and honest "thank you" near the end of your letter. Doing so will demonstrate respect for your reader's time and will give you a gold star for sincerity.

Warning—Sentence Construction Ahead

Remember all those rules in Chapter 15, "Good Technique Helps"? Now it's time to lean on them to compose coherent sentences and to connect those sentences to form paragraphs. Before you know it—*Voilà!*—your letter will be finished.

I'm not going to go deeply into sentence structure (subjects, verbs, objects, etc.) and I'm certainly not going to ask you to diagram your sentences. But you *do* need to be aware of the most common pitfalls in letter writing, which are:

> Run-on sentences
>
> Dangling clauses
>
> Misplaced modifiers
>
> Passive voice

Rule

Rule #2: Show Personality. To write a personable letter, imagine that you're having a friendly chat with your prospective boss. What would you say? How would you say it? The answers to these questions will tell you how to phrase your letter.

Ready to learn about them? Let's dive in…

Don't Let Run-On Sentences Run the Show

A run-on sentence does just what its name implies—it runs on and on like a river rambling aimlessly through the country side. Just as a traveler on a long, twisted river may lose his sense of direction, so the reader of a run-on sentence gets confused and frustrated. You don't want to do that to your next boss (the reader of your cover letter), do you?

Q & A

How can I tell if I've written a run-on sentence?

Here's a simple trick to identify a run-on: Read your sentence out loud. If you have to come up for air before reaching the end, it's probably a run-on sentence! If you have to read the sentence more than once to follow its train of thought, it's likely you have a run-on sentence.

Although you probably recognize a run-on sentence when you see one, let me give you an example, just to make sure:

> *At Westinghouse, I was assigned, and completed, a wide variety of tasks, usually on a limited budget I might add, and I have had significant success at both coming in on- or under-budget and completing the assignments on schedule, much to the satisfaction of my employer.*

Phew! That long-winded sentence is a lot to chew on! It should be broken into at least three parts, making it much easier for the reader to swallow. See how simple it is to understand the following revised version?

> *At Westinghouse, I completed a wide variety of tasks. Despite having limited budgets, I had significant success at coming in on- or under-budget. I even finished the assignments on schedule, much to the satisfaction of my employer.*

After composing your letter, go over it with a fine-tooth comb to make sure you haven't written any run-on sentences.

Hanging by a Dangling Phrase

We've all said and probably written them—I'm talking about those tricky little buggers: dangling phrases. What is a dangling phrase? When a phrase at the beginning of a sentence does not agree with the subject of the sentence, the phrase is called a *dangling phrase*. Dangling phrases are considered poor sentence structure and, therefore, should not appear in your letter.

If you're not sure what I'm talking about, check out the following examples of sentences with and without danglers.

Incorrect	Correct
After staying up all night, the bank statement was impossible to reconcile. (Did the bank statement stay up all night?)	After staying up all night, I found it impossible to reconcile the bank statement.
To meet the deadline, the data must be input quickly. (The data isn't trying to meet the deadline. I am!)	To meet the deadline, I must input the data quickly.

Anyone Find a Misplaced Modifier?

A misplaced modifier is a word or phrase positioned within a sentence in such a way that it produces unintended meaning. In fact, it may turn a serious statement into a humorous one.

Here are some misplaced modifiers to chuckle over:

I received some helpful hints on protecting my investments from my local bank. (Hmm, I guess I can't trust my bank anymore.)

I think my associate dropped the letter Jim was working on in the mailbox. (Jim was in the mailbox?)

Probably the only place a misplaced modifier belongs is in a joke. Since you're serious about getting a new job, be careful not to have a misplaced modifier in your cover letter.

Using Your Most Active, Passive, and Persuasive Voices

There's an old saying that goes like this: There are people who make things happen, people who watch things happen, and people who wonder what happened. Most employers want an employee who makes things happen. If your cover letter implies you're one of the other two types, you could be sunk.

Active verbs (as opposed to passive verbs) are the key to creating the go-getter image employers like. Let's look at what active and passive verbs are and how the active voice can make you look productive.

Be Dynamic!

A *passive verb* refers to something *happening to* someone or something—it's called "passive" because the subject of the sentence remains passive while the action is done to it. An *active verb* speaks of someone or something *making something happen*—it's called "active" because the subject of the sentence generates action. If your cover letter is loaded with active verbs, it tells the reader, in no uncertain terms, that you're a dynamo!

The following examples compare the uses of active and passive verbs.

> **Watch Out!** CAUTION
> The subject and verb of your sentence must agree, even in tricky situations like this one:
>
> *Each one of the workers earns a good salary.*
>
> Because the subject, "one," is singular, its verb, "earns," must be singular.

> **Tip**
> Put yourself in your prospective employer's shoes. Would you be impressed with someone who seemed to be somewhere in the ballpark when things happened? Probably not. As a cover letter writer, use active verbs to announce exactly how you caught the ball and scored a home run.

> **Watch Out!** CAUTION
> Multi-syllable words don't always impress. As a rule, given a choice between two words that have the same meaning, choose the shorter one. For example: The word "use" is just as meaningful as, yet less formal-sounding than "utilize."

Passive	Active
I was assigned the task of reorganizing our marketing department.	I took on the job of reorganizing our marketing department.
It was accomplished in two weeks, when such a job would usually require three months.	I really hustled because my boss said I had two weeks to do a job that usually requires three months.
The ultimate outcome of the endeavor was that sales were increased by a whopping 20 percent within two months.	I did it, and in the end, our endeavor achieved a whopping 20 percent increase in sales in just two months!

Whenever possible, use an active verb instead of a passive one (i.e., say *what you did* instead of *what was done to you*). Who made it happen? You. What happened? You reorganized the marketing department, and you did it in record time. (And, by the way, what was the result? Sales improved dramatically!)

Tricky Words and Phrases

Do you ever stumble over a word because you're not sure of its meaning or use? If your answer is "yes," I'm not surprised. Almost everyone does.

Some words and phrases in particular are frequently confused and misused. To make your life a little easier, here's a list of terms you might need to know when writing your letter.

Term	Usage	Examples
A/an	Use *a* before a word that begins with a consonant-sound; use *an* before a word that begins with a vowel-sound except the long "u" and the "h" sounds.	*a home, a desk, a user, a one-day trip, an asset, an honor, an eight-day trip*
Affect/effect	*Affect* is normally used as a verb meaning "to influence, to change." *Effect* is used as a noun to mean "the result, the impression," and is also used as a verb to mean "to bring about."	*The employee's poor behavior will not affect (change) the outcome of the sale. If all goes well, our immediate response will effect (bring about) a tremendous change. In a short time, we will know the full effect (result).*
Among/ between	Generally speaking, use *among* when referring to two or more items, people, or groups. Use *between* when speaking of only two items, people, or groups.	*That should be decided among all 12 of us. We made a deal among all three nations. Small things should be decided between the two of us. It needs to comply with the agreement between Argentina and Peru.*
Anxious/eager	Use *anxious* to mean "fearful or concerned." Use *eager* to mean "desirous, willing."	*I'm eager to sign the agreement. I'm anxious about the repercussions of the agreement.*

Term	Usage	Examples
Assure/ensure/insure	*Assure* means "to give someone confidence." *Ensure* means "to make certain." *Insure* means "to protect against loss."	*I assure you the meeting will start on time. I have taken every measure to ensure that the meeting starts on time. I will insure the property for the utmost.*
Can/may	*Can* refers to ability or power to do something. *May* implies permission or possibility.	*I can write the letter immediately after lunch. May I go into the conference room to work? I may have time this afternoon to finish the letter.*
Etc.	*Etc.* is an abbreviation for "et cetera," which means "and other things." Do not place "and" before *etc.* when using *etc.* to end a series of items.	*We ordered all the office supplies: ink cartridges, paper, pens, etc.*
Farther/further	*Farther* is used to refer to physical distance. *Further* is used to speak of figurative distance or to mean "to a greater degree" or "to a greater extent."	*The farther we drive down the road, the closer we get to our destination. Do you want me to explain it further?*
Fewer/less	*Fewer* is used with plural nouns, and refers to numbers. *Less* is used with singular nouns, and refers to degree or amount.	*We have fewer products for sale this year. We have less revenue than last year.*
In regard to	In the phrases *in regard to* and *with regard to*, there should be no "s" on the end of "regard."	*This letter is in regard to the formality of our reception.*
Its/It's	*Its* is the possessive form of "it." *It's* is a contraction meaning "it is."	*Please remove the notebook from its shelf. It's been a long time since we heard from him.*
Than/then	*Than* is used to introduce a word or phrase that is being compared. *Then* speaks of time, as in "next" or "in that time."	*Rolex watches are more expensive than Timex watches. We finished the meeting, and then went to lunch.*
Toward/towards	Although *toward* is more common, both words are correct and interchangeable.	*To see the building, look toward the right. To see the building, look towards the right.*
Unique	Use *unique* only to mean "one-of-a-kind." It does not mean "unusual."	*My software design is absolutely unique.*
Who/whom	*Who* is never used as the object of a preposition. *Whom* is always the object of a preposition.	*Who is the person we have come to meet? I am scheduled to meet with whom?*

The Least You Need to Know

➤ Don't use overly formal language in your cover letter. Instead, use friendly, yet respectful wording that initiates rapport.

➤ Use your sentence structure and choice of words to convey confidence, sincerity, and your other marketable personality traits.

➤ Run-on sentences and dangling phrases make a sentence difficult to understand and therefore should not appear in your cover letter.

➤ Active verbs (instead of passive verbs) in your sentences show that you make things happen!

➤ There are many words and short phrases that are frequently misused. To be sure you don't make a mistake, check the list of "Tricky Words and Phrases" in this chapter.

Breaking Through Writer's Block

Writer's block is common, even among professional writers. If you're staring at a blank page, not knowing what on earth to write, use the exercises in this chapter to get your creative juices flowing. In no time you'll have crafted a letter that sparks your prospective employer's interest.

Exercise 1: A Stretch of the Imagination

Have you ever read a cover letter and thought, "This is terrific! How did she ever come up with such a great marketing piece?" Writing an outstanding letter can be one of a job seeker's most challenging tasks. It takes a little writing ability and, most important, lots of "marketing imagination."

Testing Limits

Picture this: a rubber band lying limp on a table in front of you. As such, the band has no strength. Stretch it even a little and the band seems to come alive with tension. Suddenly it's a useful tool for holding things together or shooting things across the room. Stretch it to its farthest point and it feels dangerous, even scary, since you know that at any second the band could break and snap your fingers. (Ouch!) Now that you've experimented with the two extremes (flaccid and precariously tight), pull the rubber band so that it's just a little less than what you know is its limit. Play with it until you find the perfect length—just the right tension and strength for the job, without the threat of breaking.

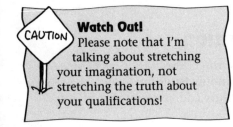

Q & A

What do you mean by "tension" in one's writing?

Tension is any aspect of your writing style or content that challenges the reader. It could be a serious stand, a humorous approach, use of slang expressions, a thought-provoking statement, or some element that is not what the reader expects.

Sharpening Your Tools

Obviously, the rubber band is my analogy for your marketing imagination. To develop a dynamite letter, stretch your marketing imagination as far as you can (yes, to the point where it seems "dangerous," or at least outlandish). Then bring it back to an appropriate point—without losing impact.

Tell It Like It Is

You're curious about what I mean by being "outlandish" with the imagination, aren't you? Here's an example of the type of brainstorming I'm talking about.

> **Watch Out!**
> Please note that I'm talking about stretching your imagination, not stretching the truth about your qualifications!

Sally was a new graduate from the University of California, Berkeley with a degree in marketing. She wanted a job in the multimedia field and she discovered Pretty Darn Smart, Inc., a company that develops interactive educational software. Let's step into Sally's mind and see how she developed a strategy for her cover letter. By the way, she had already crafted a terrific resume to go along with her letter.

I did my research on Pretty Darn Smart. They're located in Silicon Valley; employ about 50 employees, with anticipated growth to 85 before the end of the year. (Boy, I hope I'm one of them.) Their target market is private and public elementary schools throughout the U.S. Now what do you suppose they're looking for in a marketing person?

Probably somebody who:

➤ *Is smart and quick with ideas*

➤ *Knows a prospective customer when she sees one*

➤ *Jumps at opportunities*

➤ *Thinks outside the box*

➤ *Can write, and, oh yeah…*

➤ *Is a good team player*

Gee whiz, there have to be a zillion people who have these talents—not just me. How am I going to convince them to take me?

Got it! I'll use my letter as an example of my marketing abilities (meaning all those things I just mentioned). I'll prove that I'm qualified by what I say, and how I say it. Cool!

What's the craziest thing I could say?

Q & A

Why is it a good idea to have tension in my cover letter writing?

The tension created by stretching a rubber band is the force that makes the band an effective tool. Incorporating tension into one's writing is a good way to keep a reader engaged. In your job search letter, the right amount of tension can turn your letter into a "power tool."

Blurt It Out

Once Sally figured out what her potential boss wanted and how she would present her attributes, she reached for some scratch paper. Here's the outrageous, "for-her-eyes-only" draft she scribbled.

> Hey buddy,
>
> I *know* you think I'm like all the rest of those dummies in that stack of resumes you've got there, but listen—I'm different. I have pizzazz! If you pass up this opportunity, I'll sell my skills to your competition. In other words, put me on your team now or face me later on the opposing team.
>
> So call me soon… or better yet, I'll call you.
>
> Sally

Polished Rendition

Peeking into Sally's mind a little longer, let's watch how she developed her finished product.

"There, I told 'em," she said to herself as she read the rubber band draft above. "Except, I'd *never* write anything like that. But how about something with the same 'go get 'em' and 'I'm worth it' attitude. After all, isn't that what they want me to do for their product when they hire me? Sure they do!"

Toned down a smidgen, the following letter is the one Sally ultimately sent Pretty Darn Smart.

Sally Williams

0102 Ripple Road 💻 Atlanta, Georgia 13280 💻 (123) 123-1234

January 15, 199X

Mr. Alfred Price
Pretty Darn Smart, Inc.
0010 Peach Ave.
Melrose, Georgia 13281

Dear Mr. Price,

> Sally produced this highly energetic letter after writing a sassy draft that the employer never saw.

I know how urgently you want to get Pretty Darn Smart software into the hands of teachers throughout the U.S. Well, I'm eager to do the same. And with the growing competition in the educational software field, we need to join forces and get to our potential clients pretty darn quick!

That's right...I want to be your new marketing coordinator.

For nearly four years, I've been developing educational software for IntelSoft in California. In fact, as a member of Intel's development team, I worked on "Dotting Your I's," the precursor to your "SwellSpell."

With my recent move to Georgia, I've decided it's time to go back to my original career and real love: marketing.

Let's talk soon — I'm ready to hit the road running. I'll call you soon to see when I can drop by for a short visit. Thank you!

Sincerely yours,

> Word play on the company title showcases Sally's spunk.

Sally Williams

Enclosure: resume

Go Wild

When writing a first draft, experiment with marketing approaches. You want an approach that will have punch—one that demonstrates you have the skill and the personality for the job. Let your marketing imagination go wild! Be bold! Allow yourself to be completely candid, writing things frankly and without regard to how they'll be interpreted. By doing so, you'll discover what you really have to say instead of what you think you *should* say.

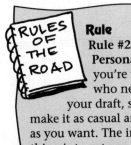

Rule

Rule #2: **Show Personality.** Usually you're the only one who needs to read your draft, so feel free to make it as casual and even crazy as you want. The important thing is to get your thoughts down on paper. You can polish the wording later.

Tip

A fictitious letter to a dear friend or relative need never be mailed. Writing such a note is just a technique for getting your thoughts onto paper.

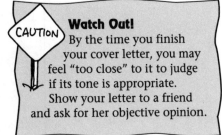

Watch Out!

By the time you finish your cover letter, you may feel "too close" to it to judge if its tone is appropriate. Show your letter to a friend and ask for her objective opinion.

Tightened Up

After completing your draft, work on the finished product, choosing which ideas should appear in the letter, and which should be left out. You may need to reword statements to make them more professional. When you do your wordsmithing, please, please use your own words and style of speaking (rather than hackneyed cover letter phrases). In other words, let your personality show!

"But," you say, "this is business correspondence. Shouldn't it sound like it?" Your letter is about business—the business of marketing you for your next job. To do that effectively, it needs to convey personality. And what if every employer doesn't like that personality? That's OK. This is one way to match yourself up with employment you'll enjoy.

Exercise 2: Dear Aunt Louise

My Aunt Louise is the most supportive and nonjudgmental person I know. I can pour my heart out to her, tell her all my dreams, moan and groan about my problems—all without any risk of tarnishing our relationship. (Yes, I've nominated Aunt Louise for sainthood.)

Talking to Aunt Louise has always been a great way for me to organize my thoughts. So sometimes when I can't think of what to say in a letter, I pull out a pad of paper and scribble a quick "note to Aunt Louise," making points to her that I want to make to the employer in my cover letter. By the time I'm done writing to Aunt Louise, I've inadvertently created a rough draft of the cover letter that had me stymied just moments before.

What's the magic behind this technique? Because I can tell Aunt Louise the unadulterated truth, which I might not dare tell an employer, my creative juices flow unbridled.

Aunt Louise doesn't care if my sentences are written perfectly or even make absolute sense. She just loves to hear from me. So I can let my thoughts spill onto the page with no worry about what she's going to think... because she doesn't judge me.

Here's the kind of letter I might write to Aunt Louise:

Dear Aunt Louise,

It seems like ages since I've seen you. Let me catch you up on the latest: I've found a great contract position and I'm going to apply for it!

Just when I'd almost given up hope that I'd ever find my dream job, I heard that Logical Processes is looking for an in-house resume consultant. Even though this sounds like I'm bragging, I can say it to you: There's no question that I'm the most qualified resume writer for the job. Here's why:

- I've authored two books on the subject.
- I've provided corporate outplacement services at some of the city's top companies.
- I have a knack for helping scared job seekers through difficult transitions.

Aunt Louise, can you picture me doing my three-hour gig in conference rooms across the country? That's right, Logical Processes is talking about contracting me for a national tour. Want to come with me? I'd love to have my best fan in the front row of every audience!

I'll keep you posted on my progress.

Love,

Susan

P.S. Please send chocolate chip cookies—sustenance for my job hunt!

Now You're Talking

Of course, I never actually mail the letter to my aunt. I change the name in the salutation to my prospective employer's name and rewrite my draft (sometimes several times) until I come up with something like the following.

Susan Ireland, Resume Writer
001 Minescape Drive ❖ San Francisco, CA 94117 ❖ (510) 558-0632

February 25, 199X

Mr. Allen Teller
Director of Human Resources
Charles Teller & Associates
001 Montgomery St., Suite 42
San Francisco, CA 94121

Using a more professional voice, this letter imitates my imaginary letter to Aunt Louise.

Dear Mr. Teller,

Re-engineering is a dreaded but sometimes necessary process in corporations. I'd like to help ease the transition your firm is going through by offering one-hour resume writing workshops and one-on-one consultations for your staff.

Here are some comments from my corporate clients:

"Using her newest book, *The Complete Idiot's Guide to the Perfect Resume,* Susan gave our employees an hour packed with valuable information." -- PG&E

"Not only is her information right-on, she delivers it superbly." -- WB Corp.

"Of all the outplacement professionals we've contracted during our recent re-engineering, Susan is the first to be recognized by the union as truly effective." -- Antioch Press

As you can gather from these quotes, I have a passion for my work. I would love to share my enthusiasm and expertise with your exiting employees. I believe I can help heal some wounds by reframing past experiences to build each participant's future.

I'll follow up on this note next week. I'd like to meet in person to discuss your plans. In the meantime, thank you for reviewing my enclosed resume.

Sincerely,

Quotes let my clients tell my reader that I'm a good presenter.

Susan Ireland

Enclosure: resume

In Aunt Louise We Trust

How does this technique help *you* overcome writer's block? Well, do you have an Aunt Louise? An Uncle Bob? Or a friend or relative who loves all your admirable and quirky traits? Someone to whom you can express yourself freely without worrying that she might disown you for a character misdemeanor? If so, write a letter to that person and consider it your cover letter draft.

To use my Aunt Louise technique, take the following steps:

1. Write a letter to Aunt Louise or one of your own dear relatives whom you trust implicitly.

2. Readdress your "Dear Aunt Louise" letter so that it is addressed to your prospective employer.

3. Rewrite the contents of the letter so that it is worded appropriately for your "next" boss, making sure that it still holds the good spirit of your draft.

Exercise 3: Third Person Scripting

Some people have the roughest time saying nice things about themselves. If you have an "I can't brag" complex, consider what someone *else* would say about you (someone who thinks you're terrific, of course). That's right, write down what your supervisor, coworker, friend, or relative might say about you… and use your notes to create a knock-out cover letter.

From the Boss

Imagine that your former or present supervisor is writing a glowing letter of recommendation about you. What do you suppose he would say? Let's find out. Pick up a piece of paper and do the following:

1. Pretend you are your boss, and think of all the things he valued (or values) about you as his employee.

2. Write a letter of recommendation that your boss might have written about you.

For example:

For family reasons, Roberta needed to leave her job at Monster Cable; and she wanted to work as a sales analyst at Fry's, one of Monster Cable's customers. She couldn't think of anything to say to Dorothy, the sales manager at Fry's, to whom her letter should

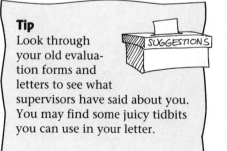

Tip
Look through your old evaluation forms and letters to see what supervisors have said about you. You may find some juicy tidbits you can use in your letter.

be sent. So she jotted down a fictitious letter of recommendation—one her boss Howard might have written to Dorothy. Here's what Howard *supposedly* said.

Ms. Dorothy Lee
Sales Manager
Fry's Electronics
3392 Grand Avenue
San Jose, CA 94228

Dear Dorothy,

My number one employee is leaving my team and she wants to join yours. I'm talking about Roberta Davis, my wonderful sales analyst for the last three years. Without her skilled number-crunching and her in-depth understanding of the consumer electronics market, I'm not sure *what* I'm going to do.

I've depended on Roberta's analyses to help me make my national and international sales decisions. In the last two years, we've climbed in revenue, despite a declining economy. How many manufacturers of peripherals can claim that? To say that Roberta deserves substantial credit for this success is an understatement.

Well, I guess if I have to lose her, I might as well lose her to you, Dorothy—my favorite customer. You run a tight ship that's laden with pressure. I assure you, Roberta meets your standards. She'll provide you with all the analyses you need to boost your financial confidence.

I hope you are well. Let's get together for coffee at the Consumer Electronics Show next month.

Sincerely

Howard Johnson

Tip

To learn how special you are on the job, talk to a trusted coworker to hear which of your shining qualities he witnessed. Ask him questions like: What achievement of mine stands out in your mind? What is the most valuable skill I contributed to the team effort? How was I better than others with similar responsibilities?

Blowing My Own Horn

Now, take your imaginary letter of recommendation and work it into a letter from *you* to your prospective employer. That's what Roberta did with her fictional letter from her boss (above). Here's the letter she finally sent to Dorothy.

Roberta Davis

001 - 45th Avenue • San Francisco, CA 94121 • (123) 123-1234

March 14, 199X

Ms. Dorothy Lee
Sales Manager
Fry's Electronics
0010 Grand Avenue
San Jose, CA 94228

Dear Dorothy,

> Having first written an imaginary letter of recommendation from her boss, Roberta found this letter easy to compose.

After so many phone conversations with you, I feel as though I know you well. Our communications are usually about business between Fry's and Monster Cable; however, this letter is of a more personal nature. I will be moving to the San Jose area in early May, and would like to speak with you about your need for a sales analyst.

At first, the idea of leaving Monster Cable was difficult for me. Then I thought of Fry's — what an ideal opportunity to transfer my skills! In addition to having proven myself in sales analysis as Howard Johnson's assistant, I have also gained more knowledge of the consumer electronics industry than a former "technophobe" ever thought she could.

I'll be in San Jose next Thursday. Are you free that day to speak in person about my working with you? I'll call you on Monday to check about a time. It will be great to see you again.

Thank you!

> Full of conversational phrases, Roberta's letter draws on her already established relationship with the reader.

Roberta Davis

Enclosure: resume

The Least You Need to Know

➤ Marketing imagination is your most valuable tool for turning out a powerful letter.

➤ Free up your creative juices by writing a preliminary draft that stretches your imagination into the absurd.

➤ Break your mental block by writing a draft addressed to a trusted relative.

➤ If you find it hard to say complimentary things about yourself in a letter, slip into someone else's shoes and think of what they would say about you.

➤ Work with your draft to produce a final version that is appropriate for the position and company to which you are applying.

Appendix

This section contains your own portfolio of dynamite cover letters. Refer to this section as you begin drafting your masterpiece. Believe me, these samples will get your creative juices flowing and help you as you:

➤ Create a letterhead and salutation that sends the right message

➤ Write an attention-grabbing lead paragraph

➤ Draft a winning pitch that convinces employers that you're the person for the job

➤ Close your letter effectively

You can find samples of fabulous broadcast letters, informational interview letters, and thank-you letters (remember the all important final touch) in "Part 4: Other Hardworking Letters."

Good luck!

PAMELA LITTLE

01 Appian Way
Sacramento, CA 95689
123/123-1234

February 1, 199X

Jim Mack, D.D.S.
001 Riverside Way, Ste. 600
Emeryville, CA 94609

A little humor starts Pamela's letter.

Dear Dr. Mack,

Imagine your office filled with clients who don't want to leave. They've strapped themselves to their chairs after getting their teeth cleaned, and they're chanting "We want more!" Or, at the very least, they're lingering by the reception desk on their way out, eager to talk about ways to improve their oral health.

We both know how many people tend to put off their regular dental appointments -- or skip them entirely, sometimes for years! Of course, this not only damages your clients' dental health; it also has a negative impact on your practice's bottom line.

As a Dental Office Manager and licensed hygienist, I specialize in providing the kind of caring, personalized service which makes a visit to the dentist more pleasant than most people ever thought possible -- *and* keeps clients coming back.

I'm eager to put my skills to use in your practice, and have several business-boosting ideas I'd like to discuss with you in person. I'll call your office next week so we can arrange a time to meet.

Thank you.

Sincerely,

By addressing Dr. Mack's bottom line, Pamela shows she understands what success means to him—and how she can help him reach it!

Pamela Little

Enclosure: resume

What a good, assertive close!

Andrew Wilmington

01 Castro Street • San Francisco, CA 94114 • 123/123-1234

July 5, 199X

Steve Rosser, Executive Director
Public Advocates, Inc.
001 Noe Street
San Francisco, CA 94117

In the middle paragraphs, Andrew pinpoints why he fits into the organization's culture and mission.

Dear Mr. Rosser,

Much of the work of an effective Administrative Director is behind the scenes. You know you have the right person in the position when you can:

- Count on your office operations running smoothly.
- Access accurate information regarding your finances at any time.
- Make efficient use of your computer hardware, software and other equipment.
- Know that your office technology is configured to meet your needs.
- Feel the team spirit in your office!

I am an experienced administrator with a strong commitment to human rights. As a gay man, I've experienced the effects of discrimination firsthand. It's important to me to work in an environment where I can use my management skills to contribute to an organization I believe in.

I am particularly attracted to Public Advocates, Inc. because of your use of both litigative and non-litigative means to correct injustice, and your emphasis on coalition-building. As a certified paralegal, I understand the essence of your work. As your Administrative Director, I will help you fulfill your agency mission.

I would enjoy speaking with you about your needs and my qualifications. I'll call your office next week to try to set a time. Thank you.

Sincerely,

Bullet points make Andrew's definition of success stand out.

Andrew Wilmington

Enclosure: resume
cc: Human Resources Department

Andrew sent a copy of his resume and cover letter to HR, as indicated by the "cc" at the bottom of the page.

Patricia Tower
123/123-1234

001 Adeline Street ◆ Berkeley, CA 94607

June 26, 199X

Human Resources Director
The Ratcliff Architects
001 Shellmound Court
Emeryville, CA 94608

This letter demonstrates how to address the Director of Human Resources.

Dear Human Resources Director,

I am an experienced bookkeeper with the background, skills and dedication to keep your firm's books just the way you need them:

- With all information clearly documented,
- All entries made in a timely manner, and
- Cross-checked so rigorously they'll pass muster in even the strictest audit.

What's more, I have the "people skills" to carry this clarity and efficiency even further. My resume details my work with project managers, assessing budgets to ensure that projects remain on-track. I'm also committed to training staff at all hierarchical levels, helping them to comply with necessary timelines and documentation.

I am eager to speak with you at greater length, and hope we will be able to schedule an appointment within the next week. I'll call your office on Wednesday to see whether you have any additional questions regarding my qualifications. Thank you.

Yours truly,

Patricia makes clear mention of her personality, which is suitable for the job she seeks.

Patricia Tower

An assertive closer keeps the ball in Patricia's court.

Enclosure: resume

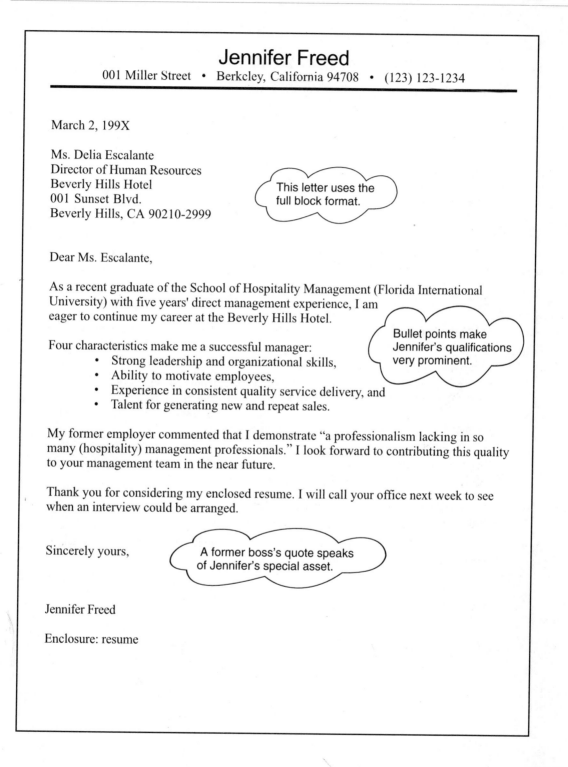

Jennifer Freed

001 Miller Street • Berkcley, California 94708 • (123) 123-1234

March 2, 199X

Ms. Delia Escalante
Director of Human Resources
Beverly Hills Hotel
001 Sunset Blvd.
Beverly Hills, CA 90210-2999

This letter uses the full block format.

Dear Ms. Escalante,

As a recent graduate of the School of Hospitality Management (Florida International University) with five years' direct management experience, I am eager to continue my career at the Beverly Hills Hotel.

Four characteristics make me a successful manager:
  • Strong leadership and organizational skills,
  • Ability to motivate employees,
  • Experience in consistent quality service delivery, and
  • Talent for generating new and repeat sales.

Bullet points make Jennifer's qualifications very prominent.

My former employer commented that I demonstrate "a professionalism lacking in so many (hospitality) management professionals." I look forward to contributing this quality to your management team in the near future.

Thank you for considering my enclosed resume. I will call your office next week to see when an interview could be arranged.

Sincerely yours,

A former boss's quote speaks of Jennifer's special asset.

Jennifer Freed

Enclosure: resume

CONNIE GEORGE
01 Divisadero Street, #100
San Francisco, CA 94123
(123) 123-1234

February 8, 199X

Ryan and Lizze Porter
The Balloon Lady
001 Market Street, Suite 250
Berkeley, CA 94202

This letter demonstrates the semiblock format.

Dear Ryan and Lizze,

I was so sorry to miss your party last Saturday. I would have loved to see you both. I'm planning another dinner in March -- I'll let you know as soon as I set the date!

Lizze, when we had lunch last fall, you mentioned you might hire a marketing director this year. Should you decide to create this position, please keep me in mind.

I am confident that my marketing skills would be an asset to your company. Here are two ideas I'd like to discuss further with you:

1. A Japanese Mail Order Program
The Japanese mail order program I designed and launched at Floressence cost less than $1000 to start up. Our most recent mailing, the Floral Holiday Gift Book, generated a 15% response, with an average order of $404. (Our domestic response rate was 2.11%, with an average order of $149.)

2. A Public Relations Program
I increased Friday Night Club's media coverage 500% over a two-year period. (PR contributed $650,000 to their yearly sales.)

If the marketing director position is not available, I would be interested in other opportunities to use my expertise in sales and marketing.

Knowing that this is a busy week for you, I'll call after Valentine's Day to see when we can get together over lunch.

Best,

Connie George

Connie's friendly style of writing incorporates the addressee's name into the body of the letter.

Enclosure: Resume

What a hook—a teaser of programs Connie has to offer her reader.

Melissa Judd
001 Laird Avenue , Oakland, CA 94605
(123) 123-1234

April 12, 199X

Ms. Anne Ward
Vice President of Marketing
Blackeyed Susan
001 MacArthur Boulevard
Oakland, CA 94602

This letter is laid out in the block format.

Dear Ms. Ward,

After meeting members of your staff through the Northern California Catalog Club and reading frequently about your company in the press, I am most enthusiastic about the prospect of putting my marketing expertise to use at Blackeyed Susan.

It's very important for me to work for a company whose product I believe in. And, having been both a customer and recipient of your floral arrangements, I'm "sold" on the service you provide!

I have a broad range of experience in circulation, along with other areas of sales and marketing. I've enclosed the award-winning catalog I compiled for L.L. Bean, together with my resume.

As a next step, may I suggest a telephone discussion about your marketing and sales challenges? I am available at the phone number listed above, and look forward to your call. Thank you.

Sincerely,

Melissa Judd

Melissa establishes a connection with the reader in her first sentence.

Enclosures: Resume
            Catalog

The second paragraph tells why Melissa fits into the reader's company.

247

Jacob Aronson

01 Jean Street
Northampton, MA 02113

123/PERFUME
123/123-1234

May 9, 199X

Here's a sample of the simplified format.

Major Cosmetics
001 Carbondale Rd.
Carbondale, IL 84730

Nice lead sentence that stimulates the employer's interest.

Re: employment opening for Director of Marketing

Why should you read my letter and resume? Because I can open the doors for you to dramatically increase your market share.

My extensive network of contacts in the perfume and cosmetics industry includes more than 1000 buyers, both domestic and international. These are professionals who know my name -- and who listen to my recommendations.

I'm poised to transfer these solid working relationships to my next position -- as your Director of Marketing.

You'll see from the enclosed resume that I have over 15 years' experience marketing products similar to yours. I'm sure you'll understand why I prefer to keep my current employer's name confidential at present, but when we meet in person, I'll gladly provide you with written documentation of my work.

I welcome your call. Thank you!

An excellent passive close that instigates action.

Jacob Aronson

Enclosure: Resume

Paul Siefert

001 Maple Street ⌨ Ann Arbor, MI 48109 ⌨ 123/123-1234

March 12, 199X

Ms. Leila Kee
Phoenix American, Inc.
001 South Park Drive
Detroit, MI 48690

Here are two good lead-in questions that compel the reader to answer "yes!"

Dear Ms. Kee,

Have you ever wished you could find a computer programmer who *really* knew how to talk to people, not just work keyboard magic?

Have you ever finished an interview with a candidate who'd looked promising on paper, and said to yourself, "Excellent communication skills, *my foot!*"?

Allow me to introduce myself -- and to resolve your dilemma. I'm a highly skilled computer programmer with a background in Alpha and Oracle Financials. I'm also a volunteer with the Big Brother/Big Sister Program, an amateur softball player and former camp counselor: in short, a well-rounded "people person."

When I combine my technical and interpersonal skills, here's what happens:

- I *accurately* assess employees' needs.
- I *directly* communicate with staff and management about budgets and timelines.
- I *incorporate* end-users' feedback and concerns throughout the programming process.
- My computer programs *work* -- helping you get your job done!

I am enthusiastic about speaking with you about how my skills can improve life at Phoenix American. For reasons of confidentiality, I would appreciate it if you could refrain from contacting my current employer until after you and I have met. I'll call you next week to arrange a mutually convenient time. Thank you!

Sincerely,

Paul uses italics and bullet points to emphasize his strengths.

Paul Siefert

Enclosure: resume

Lynn Powell
001 Pine Street, Apt. 8
Camden, NJ 30360
123-123-1234

April 29, 199X

Sr. Mary Nunes, Principal
Sisters of Mercy Junior High School
001 Waltham Way
Camden, NJ 30342

Dear Sr. Nunes,

Some people think that Catholic schools are out of step with the times. As a veteran teacher, I say just the opposite: with all the pressures teenagers are subject to these days, the discipline and values imparted by a school like Sisters of Mercy are *essential* to the well-being of our youth -- and the community at large.

Today, the problems young teens bring to the classroom are more challenging than ever before. I meet those challenges with:

• A dynamic presentation style that involves and motivates students.
• Strong classroom management skills.
• A compassionate understanding of the issues that concern youth today.

After eight years' classroom experience, I took a break to concentrate on my own family. Now that my youngest child is in high school, I'm more than ready to return to teaching.

I would like to meet with you so that we can discuss what I can offer Sisters of Mercy. I will call your office next week to arrange a time. Thank you.

Yours very truly,

Lynn Powell

Enclosure: resume

Sincerity and commitment ring loud and clear in Lynn's first paragraph.

By addressing the real issues of teaching, Lynn shows that she's ready to deal with them.

Richard Wagner
0001 Donald Way, Kansas City, KS 45632
123/123-1234

September 3, 199X

Mr. Jonathan Gold
President, Gold Building Corporation
001 Embarcadero
San Francisco, CA 94110

Dear Jonathan,

Recently, at the Midwest Builder's Conference, I had the opportunity to speak with David Hamson, who updated me on the progress of your projects in Chicago and Salt Lake City. I was pleased to hear of your continued success, as I remember well our work together on the Society Hill Towers.

I am currently planning a move back to the Bay Area, and am investigating local job prospects to see where I might make a contribution. Specifically, I see myself as providing right-hand support to the president of a development corporation.

I've enclosed my resume to give you an idea of how my career has progressed since we last saw each other. I'd like to talk with you about how I could be an asset to your development firm. I'd be grateful for a half-hour of your time one day next week, as I will be in the Bay Area from September 10-16.

I'll call your office later this week to arrange a time. I look forward to seeing you.

Regards,

Richard Wagner

Enclosure: resume

251

Ron Landstrom
Post Road #1, Box 01   Ryanstat, Wyoming 84769   (123) 123-1234

March 22, 199X

Mr. Russell Pritchard, Owner
Pritchard Veneer Manufacturing
010 Hillcrest Rd.
Billings, Wyoming 95748

This letter exudes personal and professional commitment—what more could an employer want?

Dear Mr. Pritchard,

Mr. Jacobsen first told me about your firm 13 months ago. At that time, I was absorbed in a project that kept me in international ports discovering "green" sources of eucalyptus.

Now that I've wrapped up a very productive investigation of Asian sources, I'd like to offer my expertise to you, as your Purchasing Agent.

You see, Mr. Pritchard, I share your concern that our business transactions be as healthy for the environment as they are for your bank account. Aside from the tremendous potential for profit, it is our shared environmental philosophy that sparks my interest in working for you.

I suggest we talk in person. I'll phone you next week to find a time when we are both free. Until then, thank you for perusing my enclosed resume.

Sincerely yours,

Ron clearly expresses his expertise in terms of the reader's interest and success.

Ron Landstrom

Enclosure: resume

Merl Reinsworth

001 Chatanooga Street
San Francisco, CA 94117
123/123-1234

January 12, 199X

Ms. Paulette Haste, Director
Cancer Information Service
0300 Alvarado-Niles Rd., Ste. 600
Union City, CA 94568

Merl boosts his credibility by emphasizing his personal connection with the reader's colleague.

Dear Ms. Haste,

My friend Juliette Gonzales has spoken highly of her experience at the Cancer Information Service, and suggested I contact you about your opening for Bilingual Cancer Information Specialist.

I recently returned from an extended trip to Guatemala, where I attended an intensive Spanish-language program and volunteered at an urban health clinic.

My proficiency in Spanish (particularly with health-related topics), combined with my six years' prior work in the health education field, make me a strong candidate for the position.

I am available to start immediately, and would be willing to begin on a temporar[y] part-time basis, if necessary.

I'll be in Union City next Thursday; could we meet that afternoon? I'll che[ck] you on Monday to see how your schedule looks.

Thank you!

This letter paints the picture of Merl as the perfect candidate for the job.

Sincerely,

Merl Re[insworth]

Enclosure: resume

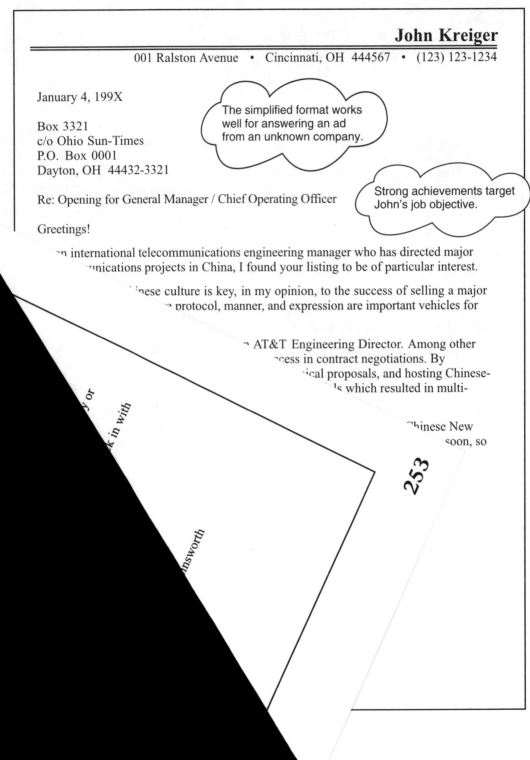

John Kreiger

001 Ralston Avenue • Cincinnati, OH 444567 • (123) 123-1234

January 4, 199X

Box 3321
c/o Ohio Sun-Times
P.O. Box 0001
Dayton, OH 44432-3321

The simplified format works well for answering an ad from an unknown company.

Re: Opening for General Manager / Chief Operating Officer

Strong achievements target John's job objective.

Greetings!

˄n international telecommunications engineering manager who has directed major
˄˄nications projects in China, I found your listing to be of particular interest.

˄nese culture is key, in my opinion, to the success of selling a major
˄ protocol, manner, and expression are important vehicles for

˄ AT&T Engineering Director. Among other
˄cess in contract negotiations. By
˄ical proposals, and hosting Chinese-
˄s which resulted in multi-

˄hinese New
˄oon, so

253

Larry Alright
001 Bay Drive • Alameda, CA 94501 • (123) 123-1234

June 10, 199X

Mr. James Afee
Personnel Director
MountainSports, Inc.
001 Broadway, #200
Seattle, WA 98010

> A polite question gets right to the point: "Do you need me?"

Dear Mr. Afee,

Are you looking for a team player with sound business sense? As a retail manager for seven years, I've perfected the art of promoting employee morale, while paying strict attention to the bottom line.

Recently I completed a 13-month solo bicycling trip through Europe. This adventure, which required organizational skills, ingenuity and flexibility (both emotional *and* physical!), deepened my commitment to working in the area of outdoor/athletics products.

I'm eager to stand behind quality products such as MountainSports', and I know I can make a contribution to your business. I will be in the Seattle area from June 10-14, and hope to speak with you in person at that time. I will call you next week to arrange an interview.

Thank you very much for your consideration.

> Larry draws on unpaid experience to demonstrate that his personality is well suited for the job.

Sincerely yours,

Larry Alright

Enclosure: resume

FLORENCE GLASSMAN, PH.D., C.P.A.

01 - 32nd Avenue • New York, NY 22145 • (123) 123-1234

July 5, 199X

Director, Regional Personnel
Hutchinson Health Care, Inc.
P.O. Box 00001
Newark, NJ 48103-3021

> Florence addressed her letter to the Director of Human Resources since she had no direct contact at the firm.

Dear Director;

In the words of former British Prime Minister Sir Winston Churchill, "The price of greatness is responsibility."

To survive and thrive in the changing U.S. health care system, Hutchinson Health Care must remain financially stable -- while continuing to provide the top-quality medical services for which you are known.

As a Hutchinson Health Care Analyst, I can help you do just that. I have a longstanding professional involvement in medical economics, and was privileged to work with three of the forerunners in the field. Our joint project was featured in the television documentary *Dollars and Sense: Rx for Healthcare.*

I've devised several long-term plans which should be of great interest to you. Shall we meet over lunch to confidentially discuss how we could work together?

Please call me at your convenience.

Yours truly,

> These achievements demonstrate that Florence is an outstanding candidate. What a good enticement for the director to call Florence.

Florence Glassman

Enclosure: resume

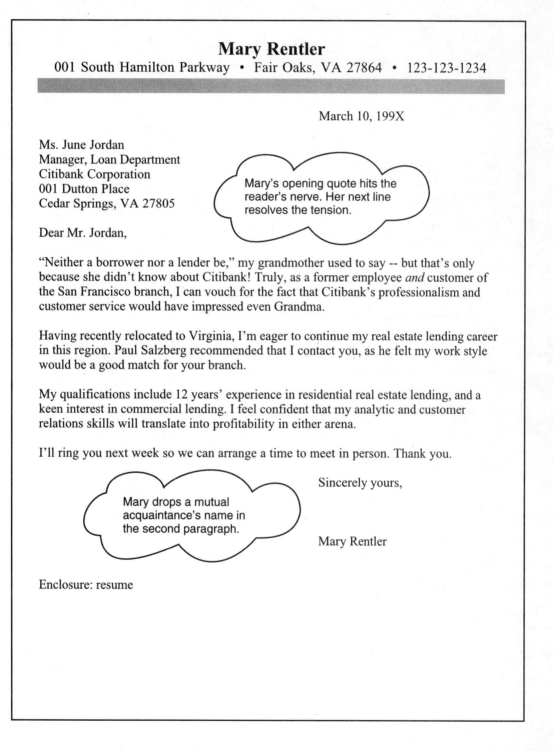

Mary Rentler
001 South Hamilton Parkway • Fair Oaks, VA 27864 • 123-123-1234

March 10, 199X

Ms. June Jordan
Manager, Loan Department
Citibank Corporation
001 Dutton Place
Cedar Springs, VA 27805

Mary's opening quote hits the reader's nerve. Her next line resolves the tension.

Dear Mr. Jordan,

"Neither a borrower nor a lender be," my grandmother used to say -- but that's only because she didn't know about Citibank! Truly, as a former employee *and* customer of the San Francisco branch, I can vouch for the fact that Citibank's professionalism and customer service would have impressed even Grandma.

Having recently relocated to Virginia, I'm eager to continue my real estate lending career in this region. Paul Salzberg recommended that I contact you, as he felt my work style would be a good match for your branch.

My qualifications include 12 years' experience in residential real estate lending, and a keen interest in commercial lending. I feel confident that my analytic and customer relations skills will translate into profitability in either arena.

I'll ring you next week so we can arrange a time to meet in person. Thank you.

Sincerely yours,

Mary drops a mutual acquaintance's name in the second paragraph.

Mary Rentler

Enclosure: resume

Donald W. English
001 Gladwyne Street ◆ Jamestown, PA 19144
123/123-1234 ◆ Email: Denglish@palcom.com

January 31, 199X

Mr. Dave McCormick
International Marketing Director
Cirrus Logic, Inc.
01 Walnut Street
Philadelphia, PA 19167

What an appropriate quote and entree for a letter to a game manufacturer!

Dear Mr. McCormick,

In the words of artist M.C. Escher, "My work is a game. A very serious game."

For myself, I would add this addendum: *And I play to win.*

I'm contacting you because I know you've got a product that deserves greater exposure -- and I've got an outstanding record in international marketing. In the past six years, I've arranged millions of dollars' worth of deals in over thirty countries.

Here's my secret: I use bold, unusual marketing strategies to achieve phenomenal results in half the expected time -- and at half the cost!

Shall we meet to discuss how we could work together? And, perhaps, for a game of chess? (I achieved statewide champion level in the 8th grade, but since that time I play only to relax -- and only after the business deals are signed!)

I'll call your office next Monday to arrange a time. I look forward to meeting you.

Yours truly,

Donald talks straight...and hits the bottom line.

Donald W. English

Enclosure: resume

Index

When You're Smart Enough to Know
That You Don't Know It All

For all the ups and downs you're sure to encounter in life, The Complete Idiot's Guides give you down-to-earth answers and practical solutions.

The Complete Idiot's Guide to Terrific Business Writing
ISBN: 0-02-861097-0 ▪ $16.95

The Complete Idiot's Guide to Winning Through Negotiation
ISBN: 0-02-861037-7 ▪ $16.95

The Complete Idiot's Guide to Managing People
ISBN: 0-02-861036-9 ▪ $18.95

The Complete Idiot's Guide to a Great Retirement
ISBN: 1-56761-601-1 ▪ $16.95

The Complete Idiot's Guide to Protecting Yourself From Everyday Legal Hassles
ISBN: 1-56761-602-X ▪ $16.99

The Complete Idiot's Guide to Surviving Divorce
ISBN: 0-02-861101-2 ▪ $16.95

The Complete Idiot's Guide to Getting the Job You Want
ISBN: 1-56761-608-9 ▪ $24.95

The Complete Idiot's Guide to Managing Your Time
ISBN: 0-02-861039-3 ▪ $14.95

The Complete Idiot's Guide to Starting Your Own Business
ISBN: 1-56761-529-5 ▪ $16.99

The Complete Idiot's Guide to Speaking in Public with Confidence
ISBN: 0-02-861038-5 ▪ $16.95

The Complete Idiot's Guide to Buying Insurance and Annuities
ISBN: 0-02-861113-6 ▪ $16.95

The Complete Idiot's Guide to Managing Your Money
ISBN: 1-56761-530-9 ▪ $16.95

Complete Idiot's Guide to Buying and Selling a Home
ISBN: 1-56761-510-4 ▪ $16.95

The Complete Idiot's Guide to Doing Your Extra Income Taxes 1996
ISBN: 1-56761-586-4 ▪ $14.99

The Complete Idiot's Guide to Making Money with Mutual Funds
ISBN: 1-56761-637-2 ▪ $16.95

The Complete Idiot's Guide to Getting Rich
ISBN: 1-56761-509-0 ▪ $16.95

You can handle it!

Look for The Complete Idiot's Guides at your favorite bookstore, or call 1-800-428-5331 for more information.

**The Complete Idiot's Guide
to Learning French on
Your Own**
ISBN: 0-02-861043-1 ▪ $16.95

**The Complete Idiot's Guide
to Dating**
ISBN: 0-02-861052-0 ▪ $14.95

**The Complete Idiot's Guide
to Hiking and Camping**
ISBN: 0-02-861100-4 ▪ $16.95

**The Complete Idiot's Guide
to Cooking Basics**
ISBN: 1-56761-523-6 ▪ $16.99

**The Complete Idiot's Guide
to Learning Spanish on
Your Own**
ISBN: 0-02-861040-7 ▪ $16.95

**The Complete Idiot's Guide
to Gambling Like a Pro**
ISBN: 0-02-861102-0 ▪ $16.95

**The Complete Idiot's Guide
to Choosing, Training, and
Raising a Dog**
ISBN: 0-02-861098-9 ▪ $16.95

The Complete Idiot's Guide to Trouble-Free Car Care
ISBN: 0-02-861041-5 ▪ $16.95

The Complete Idiot's Guide to the Perfect Wedding
ISBN: 1-56761-532-5 ▪ $16.99

The Complete Idiot's Guide to Getting and Keeping Your Perfect Body
ISBN: 0-286105122 ▪ $16.99

The Complete Idiot's Guide to the Perfect Vacation
ISBN: 1-56761-531-7 ▪ $14.99

The Complete Idiot's Guide to First Aid Basics
ISBN: 0-02-861099-7 ▪ $16.95

The Complete Idiot's Guide to Trouble-Free Home Repair
ISBN: 0-02-861042-3 ▪ $16.95

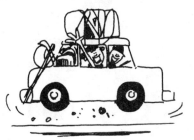

The Complete Idiot's Guide to Getting into College
ISBN: 1-56761-508-2 ▪ $14.95

You can handle it!